Volume 2
LSAT®
THE OFFICIAL TRIPLE·PREP

From the producers of the LSAT

"The most noted authority in legal publications." — *Choice*

A PUBLICATION OF

LAW SCHOOL ADMISSION COUNCIL

Contains three complete *Official PrepTests*—III (December 1991 LSAT), VI (October 1992 LSAT), VII (February 1993 LSAT)

Published by
Bantam Doubleday Dell Publishing Group, Inc.
1540 Broadway
New York, New York 10036

Library of Congress Cataloging in Publication Data
LSAT: The Official Tripleprep
p. cm.

"A publication of Law School Admission Council."

ISBN 0-385-31288-1 (v.1).—ISBN 0-385-31291-1 (v.2)

1. Law School Admission Test. 2. Law schools—United States—Admission. (U.S.) Law School Admission Council.
KF285.Z9L782 1994   94–4303
340'.076—dc20   CIP

Manufactured in the United States of America
Published simultaneously in Canada

September 1995

10 9 8 7 6 5

Table of Contents

The Law School Admission Test is a half-day standardized test required for admission to all 193 LSAC-member law schools. It consists of five 35-minute sections of multiple-choice questions. Four of the five sections contribute to the test taker's score. These sections include one reading comprehension section, one analytical reasoning section, and two logical reasoning sections. The fifth section typically is used to pretest new test items and to preequate new test forms. A 30-minute writing sample is administered at the end of the test. The writing sample is not scored by Law Services; however, copies of the writing sample are sent to all law schools to which you apply. The score scale for the LSAT is 120 to 180, with 120 being the lowest possible score and 180 the highest possible score.

The LSAT is designed to measure skills that are considered essential for success in law school: the reading and comprehension of complex texts with accuracy and insight; the organization and management of information and the ability to draw reasonable inferences from it; the ability to reason critically; and the analysis and evaluation of the reasoning and argument of others.

The LSAT provides a standard measure of acquired reading and verbal reasoning skills that law schools can use as one of several factors in assessing applicants.

Scoring

Your LSAT score is based on the number of questions you answer correctly (the raw score). There is no deduction for incorrect answers, and all questions count equally. In other words, there is no penalty for guessing.

■ Test Score Accuracy—Reliability and Standard Error of Measurement

Candidates perform at different levels on different occasions for reasons quite unrelated to the characteristics of a test itself. The accuracy of test scores is best described by the use of two related statistical terms, reliability and standard error of measurement.

Reliability is a measure of how consistently a test measures the skills under investigation. The higher the reliability coefficient for a test, the more certain we can be that test takers would get very similar scores if they took the test again.

Law Services reports an internal consistency measure of reliability for every test form. The reliability coefficient can vary from 0.00 to 1.00; a test with no measurement error would have a reliability coefficient of 1.00 (never attained in practice). In the past, reliability coefficients for LSAT forms have ranged from .90 to .95, indicating a very reliable test. Law Services expects the reliability to continue to fall within the same range.

The LSAT, like any standardized test, is not a perfect measuring instrument. One way to quantify measurement error is through calculation of the **standard error of measurement**. The standard error of measurement provides an estimate of the error that is present in a test score because of the imperfect nature of the test.

The standard error of measurement for the LSAT is reported to score users following each administration of the test. The chances are approximately two out of three that a score obtained by a test taker will lie within a range from

one standard error of measurement below to one standard error of measurement above his or her true score. The true score is the score that a test taker would have obtained if the test contained no measurement error. About 95 percent of the test takers will have test scores that fall within two standard errors of measurement of their true scores. The standard error of measurement for LSAT forms tends to be approximately 2.6.

Measurement error also must be taken into account when comparing LSAT scores of two test takers. It is likely that small differences in scores are due to measurement error rather than to meaningful differences in ability. The standard error of score differences provides some guidance as to the importance of differences between two scores. The standard error of score differences is approximately 1.4 times as large as the standard error of measurement for the individual scores.

Thus, a test score should be regarded as a useful but approximate measure of a candidate's abilities as measured by the test, not as an exact determination of his or her standing. LSAC encourages law schools to interpret LSAT scores as intervals, not as exact points on a scale.

■ Adjustments for Variation in Test Difficulty

All test forms of the LSAT reported on the same score scale are designed to measure the same abilities, but one test form may be slightly easier or more difficult than another. The scores from different test forms are made comparable through a statistical procedure known as equating. As a result of equating, a given scaled score earned on different test forms reflects the same level of ability.

■ Research on the LSAT

Summaries of LSAT validity studies and other LSAT research can be found in member law school libraries.

How the PrepTest Differs from an Actual LSAT

Each PrepTest is made up of the scored sections and writing sample from an actual LSAT. However, it does not contain the extra, variable section that is used to pre-test new test items of one of the three question types. Also, you are likely to encounter the three LSAT question types in a different order when you take an actual LSAT than in the PrepTest. This is because the order of the question types is intentionally varied for each administration of the test.

The Question Types

The multiple-choice questions that make up most of the LSAT reflect a broad range of academic disciplines and are intended to give no advantage to candidates from a particular academic background.

The five sections of the test contain three different question types. The following material presents a general discussion of the nature of each question type and some strategies that can be used in answering them.

■ Reading Comprehension Questions

The purpose of reading comprehension questions is to measure your ability to read, with understanding and insight, examples of lengthy and complex materials similar to those commonly encountered in law school work. The reading comprehension section of the test consists of four passages, each approximately 450 words long, followed by five to eight questions that test the candidate's reading and reasoning abilities. Passages for reading comprehension items draw from a variety of subjects—including the humanities, the social sciences, the physical sciences, ethics, philosophy, and the law.

Reading comprehension questions require test takers to read carefully and accurately, to determine the relationships among the various parts of the passage, and to draw reasonable inferences from the material in the passage. The questions may ask about:

- the main idea or primary purpose of the passage;

- the meaning or purpose of words or phrases used in the passage;

- information explicitly stated in the passage;

- information or ideas that can be inferred from the passage;

- the organization of the passage;

- the application of information in the passage to a new context; and

- the tone of the passage or the author's attitude as it is revealed in the language used.

Suggested Approach

Since passages are drawn from many different disciplines and sources, you should not be discouraged if you encounter material with which you are not familiar. It is important to remember that questions are to be answered on the basis of the information provided in the passage. There is no particular knowledge that you are expected to bring to the test, and you should not make inferences based on any prior knowledge of a subject that you may have. You may, however, wish to defer working on a passage that seems particularly difficult or unfamiliar until after you have dealt with passages you find easier.

Strategies. In preparing for the test, you should experiment with different strategies, and decide which work most effectively for you. These include:

- Reading the passage very closely and then answering the questions;

- Reading the questions first, reading the passage closely, and then returning to the questions; and

- Skimming the passage and questions very quickly, then rereading the passage closely and answering the questions.

Remember that your strategy must be effective under timed conditions.

Reading the passage. Whatever strategy you choose, you should give the passage at least one careful reading before answering the questions. Separate main ideas from supporting ideas and the author's own ideas or attitudes from factual, objective information. Note transitions from one idea to the next and examine the relationships among the different ideas or parts of the passage. For example, are they contrasting or complementary? Consider how and why the author makes points and draws conclusions. Be sensitive to the implications of what the passage says.

You may find it helpful to mark key parts of the passage. For example, you might underline main ideas or important arguments, and you might circle transitional words—'although,' 'nevertheless,' 'correspondingly,' and the like—that will help you map the structure of the passage. Moreover, you might note descriptive words that will help you identify the author's attitude toward a particular idea or person.

Answering the Questions

- Always read all the answer choices before selecting the best answer. The best answer choice is the one that most accurately and completely answers the question being posed.

- Respond to the specific question being asked. Do not pick an answer choice simply because it is a true statement. For example, picking a true statement might yield an incorrect answer to a question in which you are asked to identify the author's position on an issue, since here you are not being asked to evaluate the truth of the author's position, but only to correctly identify what that position is.

- Answer the questions only on the basis of the information provided in the passage. Your own views, interpretations, or opinions, and those you have heard from others, may sometimes conflict with those expressed in the passage; however, you are expected to work within the context provided by the passage. You should not expect to agree with everything you encounter in reading comprehension passages.

■ Analytical Reasoning Questions

Analytical reasoning items are designed to measure the ability to understand a structure of relationships and to draw conclusions about the structure. The examinee is asked to make deductions from a set of statements, rules, or conditions that describe relationships among entities such as persons, places, things, or events. They simulate the kinds of detailed analyses of relationships that a law student must perform in solving legal problems. For example, a passage might describe four diplomats sitting around a table, following certain rules of protocol as to who can sit where. The test taker must answer questions about the implications of the given information, for example, who is sitting between diplomats X and Y.

The passage used for each group of questions describes a common relationship such as the following:

- Assignment: Two parents, P and O, and their children, R and S, must go to the dentist on four consecutive days, designated 1, 2, 3, and 4 ...;

- Ordering: X arrived before Y but after Z;

- Grouping: A basketball coach is trying to form a lineup from seven players— R,S,T,U,V,W, and X...and each player has a particular strength—shooting, jumping, or guarding;

- Spatial: Country X contains six cities and each city is connected to at least one other city by a system of roads, some of which are one-way.

Careful reading and analysis are necessary to determine the exact nature of the relationships involved. Some relationships are fixed (e.g., P and R always sit at the same table). Other relationships are variable (e.g., Q must be assigned to either table 1 or table 3). Some relationships that are not stated in the conditions are implied by and can be deduced from those that are stated. (e.g., If one condition about books on a shelf specifies that Book L is to the left of Book Y, and another specifies that Book P is to the left of Book L, then it can be deduced that Book P is to the left of Book Y.)

No formal training in logic is required to answer these questions correctly. Analytical reasoning questions are intended to be answered using knowledge, skills, and reasoning ability generally expected of college students and graduates.

Suggested Approach

Some people may prefer to answer first those questions about a passage that seem less difficult and then those that seem more difficult. In general, it is best not to start another passage before finishing one begun earlier, because much time can be lost in returning to a passage and reestablishing familiarity with its relationships. Do not assume that, because the conditions for a set of questions look long or complicated, the questions based on those conditions will necessarily be especially difficult.

Reading the passage. In reading the conditions, do not introduce unwarranted assumptions. For instance, in a set establishing relationships of height and weight among the members of a team, do not assume that a person who is taller than another person must weigh more than that person. All the information needed to answer each question is provided in the passage and the question itself.

The conditions are designed to be as clear as possible; do not interpret them as if they were intended to trick you. For example, if a question asks how many people could be eligible to serve on a committee, consider only those people named in the passage unless directed otherwise. When in doubt, read the conditions in their most obvious sense. Remember, however, that the language in the conditions is intended to be read for precise meaning. It is essential to pay particular attention to words that describe or limit relationships, such as 'only,' 'exactly,' 'never,' 'always,' 'must be,' 'cannot be,' and the like.

The result of this careful reading will be a clear picture of the structure of the relationships involved, including the kinds of relationships permitted, the participants in the relationships, and the range of actions or attributes allowed by the relationships for these participants.

Questions are independent. Each question should be considered separately from the other questions in its group; no information, except what is given in the original conditions, should be carried over from one question to another. In some cases a question will simply ask for conclusions to be drawn from the conditions as originally given. Some questions may, however, add information to the original conditions or temporarily suspend one of the original conditions for the purpose of that question only. For example, if Question 1 adds the information "if P is sitting at table 2...," this information should NOT be carried over to any other question in the group.

Highlighting the text; using diagrams. Many people find it useful to underline key points in the passage and in each question. In addition, it may prove very helpful to draw a diagram to assist you in finding the solution to the problem.

In preparing for the test, you may wish to experiment with different types of diagrams. For a scheduling problem, a calendar-like diagram may be helpful. For a spatial relationship problem, a simple map can be a useful device.

Even though some people find diagrams to be very helpful, other people seldom use them. And among those who do regularly use diagrams in solving these problems, there is by no means universal agreement on which kind of diagram is best for which problem or in which cases a diagram is most useful. Do not be concerned if a particular problem in the test seems to be best approached without the use of a diagram.

■ Logical Reasoning Questions

Logical reasoning questions evaluate a test taker's ability to understand, analyze, criticize, and complete arguments. The arguments are contained in short passages taken from a variety of sources, including letters to the editor, speeches, advertisements, newspaper articles and editorials, informal discussions and conversations, as well as articles in the humanities, the social sciences, and the natural sciences.

Each logical reasoning question requires the examinee to read and comprehend the argument or the reasoning

contained in the passage, and answer one or two questions about it. The questions test a variety of logical skills. These include:

- recognizing the point or issue of an argument or dispute;

- detecting the assumptions involved in an argument or chain of reasoning;

- drawing reasonable conclusions from given evidence or premises;

- identifying and applying principles;

- identifying the method or structure of an argument or chain of reasoning;

- detecting reasoning errors and misinterpretations;

- determining how additional evidence or argument affects an argument or conclusion; and

- identifying explanations and recognizing resolutions of conflicting facts or arguments.

The questions do not presuppose knowledge of the terminology of formal logic. For example, you will not be expected to know the meaning of specialized terms such as "ad hominem" or "syllogism." On the other hand, you will be expected to understand and critique the reasoning contained in arguments. This requires that you possess, at a minimum, a college-level understanding of widely used concepts such as argument, premise, assumption, and conclusion.

Suggested Approach

Read each question carefully. Make sure that you understand the meaning of each part of the question. Make sure that you understand the meaning of each answer choice and the ways in which it may or may not relate to the question posed.

Do not pick a response simply because it is a true statement. Although true, it may not answer the question posed.

Answer each question on the basis of the information that is given, even if you do not agree with it. Work within the context provided by the passage. LSAT questions do not involve any tricks or hidden meanings.

The Writing Exercise

Test takers are given 30 minutes to complete the brief writing exercise, which is not scored but is used by law school admission personnel to assess writing skill. Read the topic carefully. You will probably find it best to spend a few minutes considering the topic and organizing your thoughts before you begin writing. **Do not write on a topic other than the one specified. Writing on a topic of your own choice is not acceptable.**

There is no "right" or "wrong" position on the writing sample topic. Law schools are interested in how skillfully you support the position you take and how clearly you express that position. How well you write is much more important than how much you write. No special knowledge is required or expected. Law schools are interested in organization, vocabulary, and writing mechanics. They understand the short time available to you and the pressure under which you are writing.

Confine your writing to the lined area following the writing sample topic. You will find that you have enough space if you plan your writing carefully, write on every line, avoid wide margins, and keep your handwriting a reasonable size. Be sure that your handwriting is legible.

Scratch paper is provided for use during the writing sample portion of the test only. Scratch paper cannot be used in other sections of the LSAT.

The writing sample is photocopied and sent to law schools to which you direct your LSAT score. A pen will be provided at the test center, which must be used (for the writing sample only) to ensure a photocopy of high quality.

Taking the PrepTest Under Simulated LSAT Conditions

One important way to prepare for the LSAT is to take a sample test under the same requirements and time limits you will encounter in taking an actual LSAT. This helps you to estimate the amount of time you can afford to spend on each question in a section and to determine the question types on which you may need additional practice.

Since the LSAT is a timed test, it is important to use your allotted time wisely. During the test, you may work only on the section designated by the test supervisor. You cannot devote extra time to a difficult section and make up that time on a section you find easier. In pacing yourself, and checking your answers, you should think of each section of the test as a separate minitest.

Be sure that you answer every question on the test. When you do not know the correct answer to a question, first eliminate the responses that you know are incorrect, then make your best guess among the remaining choices. Do not be afraid to guess.

When you take a sample test abide by all the requirements specified in the directions and keep strictly within the specified time limits. Work without a rest period. When you take an actual test you will have only a short break—usually 10-15 minutes—after SECTION III.

When taken under conditions as much like actual testing conditions as possible, a sample test provides very useful preparation for taking the LSAT.

Official directions for the four multiple-choice sections and the writing sample are included in this book so that you can use the PrepTests to approximate actual testing conditions as you practice.

To take a sample test:

- Set a timer for 35 minutes. Answer all the questions in SECTION I of one PrepTest. Stop working on that section when the 35 minutes have elapsed.

- Repeat, allowing yourself 35 minutes each for sections II, III, and IV.

- Set the timer for 30 minutes, then prepare your response to the writing sample for the PrepTest.

- Refer to "Computing Your Score" for that PrepTest for instruction on evaluating your performance. An answer key is provided for that purpose.

The Official

LSAT

PrepTest™ III

The sample test that follows consists of
four sections corresponding to the four
scored sections of the December 1991 LSAT.

December 1991
Form 2LSS13

INSTRUCTIONS FOR COMPLETING THE BIOGRAPHICAL AREA ARE ON THE BACK COVER OF YOUR TEST BOOKLET.
USE ONLY A NO. 2 OR HB PENCIL TO COMPLETE THIS ANSWER SHEET. DO NOT USE INK.

1   LAST NAME   FIRST NAME   MI

(Grid of bubbles A–Z for each letter position)

2   DATE OF BIRTH

MONTH	DAY	YEAR
Jan		
Feb		
Mar		
Apr		
May		
June		
July		
Aug		
Sept		
Oct		
Nov		
Dec		

3   SOCIAL SECURITY NO.

(Grid of bubbles 0–9)

Right Mark: ●
Wrong Marks: ⊘ ⊗ ⊙

4   ETHNIC DESCRIPTION

- American Indian/ Alaskan Native
- Asian/Pacific Islander
- Black/African Amer.
- Canadian Aboriginal
- Caucasian/White
- Chicano/Mex. Amer.
- Hispanic
- Puerto Rican
- Other

5   GENDER

- Male
- Female

6   DOMINANT LANGUAGE

- English
- Other

7   ENGLISH FLUENCY

- Yes
- No

8   CENTER NUMBER

(Grid of bubbles 0–9)

9   TEST FORM CODE

(Grid of bubbles 0–9)

10   TEST BOOK SERIAL NO.

11   TEST FORM

12   TEST DATE

MONTH   DAY   YEAR

13   PLEASE PRINT ALL INFORMATION

LAST NAME   FIRST

MAILING ADDRESS

SOCIAL SECURITY/ SOCIAL INSURANCE NO.

LAW SCHOOL ADMISSION TEST

MARK ONE AND ONLY ONE ANSWER TO EACH QUESTION. BE SURE TO FILL IN COMPLETELY THE SPACE FOR YOUR INTENDED ANSWER CHOICE. IF YOU ERASE, DO SO COMPLETELY. MAKE NO STRAY MARKS.

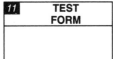
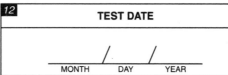

SECTION 1 | **SECTION 2** | **SECTION 3** | **SECTION 4** | **SECTION 5**

(Each section contains questions 1–30 with answer choices A B C D E)

NOTE: If you have a new address, you must write Law Services at Box 2000-C, Newtown, PA 18940 or call (215) 968-1001. We cannot guarantee that all address changes will be processed before scores are mailed, so be sure to notify your post office of your forwarding address.

FOR LAW SERVICES USE ONLY		
LR		
LW		
LCS		

General Directions for the LSAT Answer Sheet

The actual testing time for this portion of the test will be 2 hours 55 minutes. There are five sections, each with a time limit of 35 minutes. The supervisor will tell you when to begin and end each section. If you finish a section before time is called, you may check your work on that section <u>only</u>; do not turn to any other section of the test book and do not work on any other section either in the test book or on the answer sheet.

There are several different types of questions on the test, and each question type has its own directions. <u>Be sure you understand the directions for each question type before attempting to answer any questions in that section.</u>

Not everyone will finish all the questions in the time allowed. Do not hurry, but work steadily and as quickly as you can without sacrificing accuracy. You are advised to use your time effectively. If a question seems too difficult, go on to the next one and return to the difficult question after completing the section. MARK THE BEST ANSWER YOU CAN FOR EVERY QUESTION. NO DEDUCTIONS WILL BE MADE FOR WRONG ANSWERS. YOUR SCORE WILL BE BASED ONLY ON THE NUMBER OF QUESTIONS YOU ANSWER CORRECTLY.

ALL YOUR ANSWERS MUST BE MARKED ON THE ANSWER SHEET. Answer spaces for each question are lettered to correspond with the letters of the potential answers to each question in the test book. After you have decided which of the answers is correct, blacken the corresponding space on the answer sheet. BE SURE THAT EACH MARK IS BLACK AND COMPLETELY FILLS THE ANSWER SPACE. Give only one answer to each question. If you change an answer, be sure that all previous marks are <u>erased completely</u>. Since the answer sheet is machine scored, incomplete erasures may be interpreted as intended answers. ANSWERS RECORDED IN THE TEST BOOK WILL NOT BE SCORED.

There may be more questions noted on this answer sheet than there are questions in a section. Do not be concerned but be certain that the section and number of the question you are answering matches the answer sheet section and question number. Additional answer spaces in any answer sheet section should be left blank. Begin your next section in the number one answer space for that section.

Score Cancellation

Complete this section only if you are absolutely certain you want to cancel your score. A CANCELLATION REQUEST CANNOT BE RESCINDED. IF YOU ARE AT ALL UNCERTAIN, YOU SHOULD NOT COMPLETE THIS SECTION; INSTEAD, YOU SHOULD USE THE TIME ALLOWED AFTER THE TEST (UP TO 5 DAYS) TO FULLY CONSIDER YOUR DECISION.

To cancel your score from this administration, you must:

A.   fill in the ovals here........ ◯ ◯

B.   read the following statement. Then sign your name and enter the date.

I certify that I wish to cancel my test score from this administration. I understand that my request is irreversible and that my score will not be sent to me or to the law schools to which I apply.

_____
Sign your name in full

_____
Date

HOW DID YOU PREPARE FOR THE LSAT?
(Select all that apply.)

Responses to this item are voluntary and will be used for statistical research purposes only.

◯ By studying the sample questions in the *LSAT/LSDAS Registration and Information Book.*
◯ By taking the free sample LSAT.
◯ By working through *The Official LSAT PrepTest(s), PrepBook, Workbooks, or PrepKit.*
◯ By using a book on how to prepare for the LSAT **not** published by Law Services.
◯ By attending a commercial test preparation or coaching course.
◯ By attending a test preparation or coaching course offered through an undergraduate institution.
◯ Self study.
◯ Other preparation.
◯ No preparation.

CERTIFYING STATEMENT

Please write (DO NOT PRINT) the following statement. Sign and date.

I certify that I am the examinee whose name appears on this answer sheet and that I am here to take the LSAT for the sole purpose of being considered for admission to law school. I further certify that I will neither assist nor receive assistance from any other candidate, and I agree not to copy or retain examination questions or to transmit them in any form to any other person.

_____
_____
_____
_____
_____
_____
_____
_____
_____

SIGNATURE: _____   TODAY'S DATE: _____ / _____ / _____
                                                                          MONTH DAY YEAR

SECTION I

Time—35 minutes

24 Questions

Directions: Each group of questions in this section is based on a set of conditions. In answering some of the questions, it may be useful to draw a rough diagram. Choose the response that most accurately and completely answers each question and blacken the corresponding space on your answer sheet.

Questions 1–7

Three couples—John and Kate, Lewis and Marie, and Nat and Olive—have dinner in a restaurant together. Kate, Marie, and Olive are women; the other three are men. Each person orders one and only one of the following kinds of entrees: pork chops, roast beef, swordfish, tilefish, veal cutlet. The six people order in a manner consistent with the following conditions:

 The two people in each couple do not order the same kind of entree as each other.

 None of the men orders the same kind of entree as any of the other men.

 Marie orders swordfish.

 Neither John nor Nat orders a fish entree.

 Olive orders roast beef.

1. Which one of the following is a complete and accurate list of the entrees any one of which Lewis could order?

 (A) pork chops, roast beef
 (B) pork chops, veal cutlet
 (C) pork chops, swordfish, veal cutlet
 (D) pork chops, roast beef, tilefish, veal cutlet
 (E) pork chops, roast beef, swordfish, tilefish, veal cutlet

2. Which one of the following statements could be true?

 (A) John orders the same kind of entree as Marie does.
 (B) Kate orders the same kind of entree as Nat does.
 (C) Lewis orders the same kind of entree as Nat does.
 (D) Marie orders the same kind of entree as Olive does.
 (E) Nat orders the same kind of entree as Olive does.

3. Which one of the following statements must be true?

 (A) One of the men orders pork chops or veal cutlet.
 (B) One of the men orders swordfish or veal cutlet.
 (C) Two of the women order tilefish.
 (D) None of the men orders a fish entree.
 (E) Exactly one of the women orders a fish entree.

4. If John orders veal cutlet, then which one of the following statements must be true?

 (A) Kate orders roast beef.
 (B) Kate orders swordfish.
 (C) Lewis orders tilefish.
 (D) Lewis orders veal cutlet.
 (E) Nat orders pork chops.

5. If none of the six people orders pork chops, then which one of the following statements must be true?

 (A) John orders veal cutlet.
 (B) Kate orders tilefish.
 (C) Lewis orders tilefish.
 (D) One of the men orders swordfish.
 (E) One of the women orders tilefish.

6. If Lewis orders pork chops, then which one of the following is a complete and accurate list of the entrees any one of which John could order?

 (A) roast beef
 (B) veal cutlet
 (C) roast beef, veal cutlet
 (D) roast beef, swordfish
 (E) pork chops, roast beef, swordfish

7. Suppose that the people in each couple both order the same kind of entree as each other rather than order different kinds of entrees. If all other conditions remain the same, and no two women order the same kind of entree, then which one of the following statements could be true?

 (A) John orders roast beef.
 (B) John orders swordfish.
 (C) Kate orders roast beef.
 (D) Two of the people order pork chops.
 (E) Two of the people order tilefish.

GO ON TO THE NEXT PAGE.

Questions 8–13

There are exactly seven houses on a street. Each house is occupied by exactly one of seven families: the Kahns, Lowes, Muirs, Newmans, Owens, Piatts, Rutans. All the houses are on the same side of the street, which runs from west to east.

The Rutans do not live in the first or the last house on the street.

The Kahns live in the fourth house from the west end of the street.

The Muirs live next to the Kahns.

The Piatts live east of both the Kahns and the Muirs but west of the Lowes.

8. Which one of the following families could live in the house that is the farthest east?

(A) the Kahns
(B) the Muirs
(C) the Newmans
(D) the Piatts
(E) the Rutans

9. Which one of the following families CANNOT live next to the Kahns?

(A) the Lowes
(B) the Newmans
(C) the Owens
(D) the Piatts
(E) the Rutans

10. If the Muirs live west of the Kahns, then the Rutans CANNOT live next to both

(A) the Kahns and the Piatts
(B) the Lowes and the Piatts
(C) the Muirs and the Piatts
(D) the Muirs and the Owens
(E) the Muirs and the Newmans

11. If the Newmans live immediately west of the Kahns, which one of the following statements must be false?

(A) The Owens live next to the Newmans.
(B) The Owens live next to the Rutans.
(C) The Piatts live next to the Lowes.
(D) The Piatts live next to the Muirs.
(E) The Rutans live next to the Newmans.

12. If the Owens live east of the Muirs, which one of the following statements must be true?

(A) The Kahns live east of the Muirs.
(B) The Kahns live west of the Rutans.
(C) The Owens live west of the Lowes.
(D) The Owens live east of the Piatts.
(E) The Owens live west of the Piatts.

13. If the Owens live east of the Kahns, which one of the following pairs of families must live next to each other?

(A) the Kahns and the Piatts
(B) the Lowes and the Owens
(C) the Muirs and the Newmans
(D) the Newmans and the Rutans
(E) the Owens and the Piatts

GO ON TO THE NEXT PAGE.

Questions 14–19

At an automobile exhibition, cars are displayed on each floor of a three-floor building. On each floor the cars are either all family cars or all sports cars, either all new or all used, and either all production models or all research models. The following conditions apply to this exhibition:

If the exhibition includes both family cars and sports cars, then each family car is displayed on a lower-numbered floor than any sports car.

The exhibition includes no used research models.

The exhibition includes no research models that are sports cars.

There are new cars on floor 1.

There are used cars on floor 3.

14. If there are sports cars on exactly two floors, then which one of the following statements could be true?

   (A) There are research models on floor 1.
   (B) There are sports cars on floor 1.
   (C) There are family cars on floor 2.
   (D) There are research models on floor 2.
   (E) There are family cars on floor 3.

15. Which one of the following statements could be true?

   (A) The exhibition includes new research model sports cars.
   (B) The exhibition includes used research model family cars.
   (C) The exhibition includes used research model sports cars.
   (D) There are research models on exactly one floor.
   (E) There are research models on all three floors.

16. Which one of the following statements must be true?

   (A) There are production models on floor 1.
   (B) There are research models on floor 1.
   (C) There are production models on floor 2.
   (D) There are production models on floor 3.
   (E) There are research models on floor 3.

17. If there are research models on exactly two floors, then which one of the following statements can be false?

   (A) There are family cars on floor 1.
   (B) There are research models on floor 1.
   (C) There are new cars on floor 2.
   (D) There are research models on floor 2.
   (E) There are family cars on floor 3.

18. If all the new cars in the exhibition are research models, then which one of the following statements must be true?

   (A) All the family cars in the exhibition are new.
   (B) All the family cars in the exhibition are research models.
   (C) All the family cars in the exhibition are used.
   (D) All the new cars in the exhibition are family cars.
   (E) All the production models in the exhibition are family cars.

19. If all the production models in the exhibition are used, then which one of the following statements must be true?

   (A) There are family cars on floor 1.
   (B) There are new cars on floor 2.
   (C) There are research models on floor 2.
   (D) There are family cars on floor 3.
   (E) There are sports cars on floor 3.

GO ON TO THE NEXT PAGE.

Questions 20–24

Planes 1, 2, 3, and 4—and no others—are available to fly in an air show.

   Pilots Anna, Bob, and Cindy are all aboard planes that are flying in the show and they are the only qualified pilots in the show.

   Copilots Dave, Ed, and Fran are all aboard planes that are flying in the show and they are the only qualified copilots in the show.

   No plane flies in the show without a qualified pilot aboard.

   No one but qualified pilots and qualified copilots flies in the show.

   Anna will only fly in either plane 1 or plane 4.

   Dave will only fly in either plane 2 or plane 3.

20. If Anna flies in plane 4 and Dave flies in plane 2, which one of the following must be true?

   (A)   Cindy flies in either plane 1 or plane 3.
   (B)   If Cindy flies in plane 3, Bob flies in plane 2.
   (C)   Bob and one other person fly in plane 1.
   (D)   If Bob is aboard plane 4, Cindy flies in plane 3.
   (E)   If Cindy is in plane 2, Bob flies in plane 3.

21. If Bob and Anna fly on the same plane, which one of the following must be true?

   (A)   Cindy flies with Dave and Ed.
   (B)   Cindy flies with Ed.
   (C)   Dave flies with Cindy.
   (D)   Dave flies with Cindy, Ed, and Fran.
   (E)   Fran flies with Ed.

22. If Cindy and Fran are the only people in one of the planes, which one of the following must be true?

   (A)   Bob flies with Anna.
   (B)   Dave flies with Ed.
   (C)   Dave and Ed fly with Bob.
   (D)   Dave flies with Bob.
   (E)   Ed flies with Anna.

23. If plane 1 is used, its crew could consist of

   (A)   Anna, Bob, Cindy, Fran
   (B)   Anna, Bob, Ed, Fran
   (C)   Bob, Cindy, Ed, Fran
   (D)   Bob, Cindy, Dave, Ed
   (E)   Bob, Dave, Ed, Fran

24. If as many of the pilots and copilots as possible fly in plane 4, that group will consist of

   (A)   exactly two people
   (B)   exactly three people
   (C)   exactly four people
   (D)   exactly five people
   (E)   three pilots and two copilots

S T O P

IF YOU FINISH BEFORE TIME IS CALLED, YOU MAY CHECK YOUR WORK ON THIS SECTION ONLY.
DO NOT WORK ON ANY OTHER SECTION IN THE TEST.

SECTION II

Time—35 minutes

25 Questions

<u>Directions:</u> The questions in this section are based on the reasoning contained in brief statements or passages. For some questions, more than one of the choices could conceivably answer the question. However, you are to choose the <u>best</u> answer; that is, the response that most accurately and completely answers the question. You should not make assumptions that are by commonsense standards implausible, superfluous, or incompatible with the passage. After you have chosen the best answer, blacken the corresponding space on your answer sheet.

1. If you have a large amount of money in the bank, your spending power is great. If your spending power is great, you are happy. So if you have a large amount of money in the bank, you are happy.

    Which one of the following most closely parallels the reasoning in the argument above?

    (A) If you have good health, you can earn a lot. If you can earn a lot, you can buy an expensive house. So if you have good health, you can have a comfortable life.
    (B) If you drink too much alcohol, you will feel sick. If you drink too much alcohol, you will have no money left. So if you have no money left, you will feel sick.
    (C) If you swim energetically, your heart rate increases. If your heart rate increases, you are overexcited. So if you swim energetically, you are overexcited.
    (D) If you take a great deal of exercise, you are physically fit. If you take a great deal of exercise, you are exhausted. So if you are physically fit, you are exhausted.
    (E) If you have a large amount of money in the bank, you are confident about the future. If you are optimistic by nature, you are confident about the future. So if you have a large amount of money in the bank, you are optimistic by nature.

2. For a television program about astrology, investigators went into the street and found twenty volunteers born under the sign of Gemini who were willing to be interviewed on the program and to take a personality test. The test confirmed the investigators' personal impressions that each of the volunteers was more sociable and extroverted than people are on average. This modest investigation thus supports the claim that one's astrological birth sign influences one's personality.

    Which one of the following, if true, indicates the most serious flaw in the method used by the investigators?

    (A) The personality test was not administered or scored personally by the investigators.
    (B) People born under astrological signs other than Gemini have been judged by astrologers to be much less sociable than those born under Gemini.
    (C) The personal impressions the investigators first formed of other people have tended to be confirmed by the investigators' later experience of those people.
    (D) There is not likely to be a greater proportion of people born under the sign of Gemini on the street than in the population as a whole.
    (E) People who are not sociable and extroverted are not likely to agree to participate in such an investigation.

GO ON TO THE NEXT PAGE.

3. In Europe, schoolchildren devote time during each school day to calisthenics. North American schools rarely offer a daily calisthenics program. Tests prove that North American children are weaker, slower, and shorter-winded than European children. We must conclude that North American children can be made physically fit only if they participate in school calisthenics on a daily basis.

Which one of the following is assumed in the passage?

(A) All children can be made physically fit by daily calisthenics.
(B) All children can be made equally physically fit by daily calisthenics.
(C) Superior physical fitness produces superior health.
(D) School calisthenics are an indispensable factor in European children's superior physical fitness.
(E) North American children can learn to eat a more nutritious diet as well as to exercise daily.

4. A work of architecture, if it is to be both inviting and functional for public use, must be unobtrusive, taking second place to the total environment. Modern architects, plagued by egoism, have violated this precept. They have let their strong personalities take over their work, producing buildings that are not functional for public use.

Which one of the statements below follows logically from the statements in the passage?

(A) Unobtrusive architecture is both inviting and functional.
(B) Modern architects who let their strong personalities take over their work produce buildings that are not unobtrusive.
(C) An architect with a strong personality cannot produce buildings that function well for the public.
(D) A work of architecture that takes second place to the environment functions well for public use.
(E) A work of architecture cannot simultaneously express its architect's personality and be functional for public use.

5. Observatory director: Some say that funding the megatelescope will benefit only the astronomers who will work with it. This dangerous point of view, applied to the work of Maxwell, Newton, or Einstein, would have stifled their research and deprived the world of beneficial applications, such as the development of radio, that followed from that research.

If the statements above are put forward as an argument in favor of development of the megatelescope, which one of the following is the strongest criticism of that argument?

(A) It appeals to the authority of experts who cannot have known all the issues involved in construction of the megatelescope.
(B) It does not identify those opposed to development of the megatelescope.
(C) It launches a personal attack on opponents of the megatelescope by accusing them of having a dangerous point of view.
(D) It does not distinguish between the economic and the intellectual senses of "benefit."
(E) It does not show that the proposed megatelescope research is worthy of comparison with that of eminent scientists in its potential for applications.

6. The Transit Authority's proposal to increase fares by 40 percent must be implemented. Admittedly, this fare increase will impose a hardship on some bus and subway riders. But if the fare is not increased, service will have to be cut severely and that would result in an unacceptably large loss of ridership.

The passage employs which one of the following argumentative strategies?

(A) It offers evidence that the recommended course of action would have no undesirable consequences.
(B) It shows that a proponent of any alternative position would be forced into a contradiction.
(C) It arrives at its conclusion indirectly by providing reasons for rejecting an alternative course of action.
(D) It explains why the recommended course of action would not be subject to the objections raised against the alternative.
(E) It justifies the conclusion by showing that such a course of action has proven effective in the past.

GO ON TO THE NEXT PAGE.

7. Those who participate in local politics include people who are genuinely interested in public service and people who are selfish opportunists. Everyone who participates in local politics has an influence on the community's values.

If the statements above are true, which one of the following must also be true?

(A) Some selfish opportunists have an influence on the community's values.

(B) Some persons who are interested in public service do not have an influence on the community's values.

(C) All those who have an influence on the community's values participate in local politics.

(D) Some of those who influence the community's values neither are interested in public service nor are selfish opportunists.

(E) All those who have an influence on the community's values are either interested in public service or are selfish opportunists.

Questions 8–9

Although nondairy coffee lighteners made with coconut oil contain 2 grams of saturated fat per tablespoon, or 7 times more than does whole milk, those lighteners usually contain no cholesterol. Yet one tablespoon of such lighteners causes the consumer's blood cholesterol to rise to a higher level than does an identical amount of whole milk, which contains 2 milligrams of cholesterol per tablespoon.

8. Which one of the following, if true, contributes most to an explanation of the apparent discrepancy noted above?

(A) Nutritionists recommend that adults consume as little saturated fat as possible and no more than 250 milligrams of cholesterol a day.

(B) One gram of saturated fat in food has roughly the same effect on blood cholesterol as 25 milligrams of cholesterol in food.

(C) Light cream, a dairy product that contains 5 times more cholesterol than does whole milk, is often chosen as a lightener by consumers who normally prefer whole milk.

(D) Certain nondairy coffee lighteners made without coconut oil contain less saturated fat and less cholesterol than does whole milk.

(E) The lower the saturated fat content of dairy products, the less cholesterol they usually contain.

9. Manufacturers of coffee lighteners based on coconut oil claim that their products usually cause the typical consumer's blood cholesterol to rise to a lower level than does the use of whole milk as a lightener. Which one of the following, if true, provides the most support for the manufacturers' claim?

(A) Consumers of lighteners made with coconut oil who avoid other high-cholesterol foods and exercise more than average tend to have lower-than-average blood cholesterol levels.

(B) Coffee is frequently consumed with pastries and other rich desserts that themselves result in high blood cholesterol levels.

(C) One popular nondairy coffee lightener that is not based on coconut oil has reduced its fat content by 20 percent while keeping its cholesterol content at zero.

(D) Consumers typically add to their coffee substantially smaller quantities of coconut-oil-based lighteners than of whole milk.

(E) Most consumers are convinced that whole dairy products increase blood cholesterol and that nondairy coffee lighteners do not.

GO ON TO THE NEXT PAGE.

10. People with serious financial problems are so worried about money that they cannot be happy. Their misery makes everyone close to them—family, friends, colleagues—unhappy as well. Only if their financial problems are solved can they and those around them be happy.

Which one of the following statements can be properly inferred from the passage?

(A) Only serious problems make people unhappy.
(B) People who solve their serious financial problems will be happy.
(C) People who do not have serious financial problems will be happy.
(D) If people are unhappy, they have serious financial problems.
(E) If people are happy, they do not have serious financial problems.

11. It is often said that people should be rewarded for doing a given job in proportion to the effort it costs them to do it. However, a little reflection will show that this is, in fact, a very bad idea, since it would mean that those people with the least skill or natural aptitude for a particular task would be the ones given the most incentive to do it.

Which one of the following argumentative strategies is used above?

(A) stating a general principle and then presenting reasons in favor of adopting it
(B) providing evidence that where the principle under discussion has been adopted, the results usually have been undesirable
(C) demonstrating that a consequence that had been assumed to follow from the principle under consideration need not follow from it
(D) attempting to undermine a general principle by arguing that undesirable consequences would follow from it
(E) showing that, in practice, the principle under consideration could not be uniformly applied

12. Photovoltaic power plants produce electricity from sunlight. As a result of astonishing recent technological advances, the cost of producing electric power at photovoltaic power plants, allowing for both construction and operating costs, is one-tenth of what it was 20 years ago, whereas the corresponding cost for traditional plants, which burn fossil fuels, has increased. Thus, photovoltaic power plants offer a less expensive approach to meeting demand for electricity than do traditional power plants.

The conclusion of the argument is properly drawn if which one of the following is assumed?

(A) The cost of producing electric power at traditional plants has increased over the past 20 years.
(B) Twenty years ago, traditional power plants were producing 10 times more electric power than were photovoltaic plants.
(C) None of the recent technological advances in producing electric power at photovoltaic plants can be applied to producing power at traditional plants.
(D) Twenty years ago, the cost of producing electric power at photovoltaic plants was less than 10 times the cost of producing power at traditional plants.
(E) The cost of producing electric power at photovoltaic plants is expected to decrease further, while the cost of producing power at traditional plants is not expected to decrease.

13. If that insect is a bee, it can only sting once. It only did sting once. So it is a bee.

Which one of the following exhibits a pattern of reasoning most similar to that in the argument above?

(A) Spring is here. It has to be, because when it is spring, I cannot stop sneezing; and I just sneezed.
(B) When the sky is clear, the atmospheric pressure is high. At the moment, it is clearing up, so the atmospheric pressure is bound to be high soon.
(C) Old and brittle paintings are always moved with extreme care. That particular painting is never moved with extreme care. So it must not be old and brittle.
(D) Only one more thunderstorm was needed to ruin that roof. But the roof was still fine a month later. There must not have been any thunderstorms over that month.
(E) To survive in the wild requires physical stamina like Mark's. All the same, Mark's fear of spiders would prevent his survival.

GO ON TO THE NEXT PAGE.

14. Pamela: Physicians training for a medical specialty serve as resident staff physicians in hospitals. They work such long hours—up to 36 consecutive hours—that fatigue impairs their ability to make the best medical decisions during the final portion of their shifts.

Quincy: Thousands of physicians now practicing have been trained according to the same regimen, and records show they generally made good medical decisions during their training periods. Why should what has worked in the past be changed now?

Which one of the following, if true, is the most effective counter Pamela might make to Quincy's argument?

(A) The basic responsibilities of resident staff physicians in hospitals have not changed substantially over the past few decades.
(B) Because medical reimbursement policies now pay for less recuperation time in hospitals, patients in hospitals are, on the average, more seriously ill during their stays than in the past.
(C) It is important that emergency-room patients receive continuity of physician care, insofar as possible, over the critical period after admission, generally 24 hours.
(D) The load of work on resident physicians-in-training varies according to the medical specialty for which each is being trained.
(E) The training of physicians should include observation and recognition of the signs indicating a hospitalized patient's progress or decline over a period of at least 36 hours.

15. When a group of children who have been watching television programs that include acts of violence is sent to play with a group of children who have been watching programs that do not include acts of violence, the children who have been watching violent programs commit a much greater number of violent acts in their play than do the children who have been watching nonviolent programs. Therefore, children at play can be prevented from committing violent acts by not being allowed to watch violence on television.

The argument in the passage assumes which one of the following?

(A) Television has a harmful effect on society.
(B) Parents are responsible for the acts of their children.
(C) Violent actions and passive observation of violent actions are not related.
(D) There are no other differences between the two groups of children that might account for the difference in violent behavior.
(E) Children who are treated violently will respond with violence.

16. It is repeatedly claimed that the dumping of nuclear waste poses no threat to people living nearby. If this claim could be made with certainty, there would be no reason for not locating sites in areas of dense population. But the policy of dumping nuclear waste only in the more sparsely populated regions indicates, at the very least, some misgiving about safety on the part of those responsible for policy.

Which one of the following, if true, would most seriously weaken the argument?

(A) Evacuation plans in the event of an accident could not be guaranteed to work perfectly except where the population is small.
(B) In the event of an accident, it is certain that fewer people would be harmed in a sparsely populated than in a densely populated area.
(C) Dumping of nuclear waste poses fewer economic and bureaucratic problems in sparsely populated than in densely populated areas.
(D) There are dangers associated with chemical waste, and it, too, is dumped away from areas of dense population.
(E) Until there is no shred of doubt that nuclear dumps are safe, it makes sense to situate them where they pose the least threat to the public.

17. A society's infant mortality rate is an accepted indicator of that society's general health status. Even though in some localities in the United States the rate is higher than in many developing countries, in the United States overall the rate has been steadily declining. This decline does not necessarily indicate, however, that babies in the United States are now, on the average, healthier at birth than they were in the past.

Which one of the following reasons, if true, most strongly supports the claim made above about the implications of the decline?

(A) The figure for infant mortality is compiled as an overall rate and thus masks deficiencies in particular localities.
(B) Low birth weight is a contributing factor in more than half of the infant deaths in the United States.
(C) The United States has been developing and has achieved extremely sophisticated technology for saving premature and low-birth-weight babies, most of whom require extended hospital stays.
(D) In eleven states of the United States, the infant mortality rate declined last year.
(E) Babies who do not receive adequate attention from a caregiver fail to thrive and so they gain weight slowly.

GO ON TO THE NEXT PAGE.

Questions 18–19

Like a number of other articles, Ian Raghnall's article relied on a recent survey in which over half the couples applying for divorces listed "money" as a major problem in their marriages. Raghnall's conclusion from the survey data is that financial problems are the major problem in marriages and an important factor contributing to the high divorce rate. Yet couples often express other types of marital frustrations in financial terms. Despite appearances, the survey data do not establish that financial problems are the major problem in contemporary marriages.

18. Which one of the following sentences best expresses the main point of the passage?

(A) Financial problems are not an important factor contributing to the divorce rate.
(B) Marital problems are more easily solved by marriage counselors than by married couples on their own.
(C) The conclusion drawn in Raghnall's article is inadequately justified.
(D) Over half the couples applying for divorces listed money as a major problem in their marriages.
(E) Many articles wrongly claim that financial problems are the major factor contributing to the divorce rate.

19. In the passage, the author does which one of the following?

(A) undermines a conclusion drawn from statistical data by offering a specific counterexample
(B) undermines a conclusion drawn from statistical data by offering an alternative explanation for some of the data
(C) undermines a conclusion drawn from statistical data by showing that one cannot prove the presence of an emotion by using statistical methods
(D) undermines a conclusion drawn from statistical data by criticizing the survey for which the data was gathered
(E) undermines a conclusion by showing that couples cannot accurately describe their own problems

20. In Brazil, side-by-side comparisons of Africanized honeybees and the native honeybees have shown that the Africanized bees are far superior honey producers. Therefore, there is no reason to fear that domestic commercial honey production will decline in the United States if local honeybees are displaced by Africanized honeybees.

Each of the following, if true, would weaken the argument EXCEPT:

(A) The honeybees native to Brazil are not of the same variety as those most frequently used in the commercial beekeeping industry in the United States.
(B) Commercial honey production is far more complicated and expensive with Africanized honeybees than it is with the more docile honeybees common in the United States.
(C) If Africanized honeybees replace local honeybees, certain types of ornamental trees will be less effectively pollinated.
(D) In the United States a significant proportion of the commercial honey supply comes from hobby beekeepers, many of whom are likely to abandon beekeeping with the influx of Africanized bees.
(E) The area of Brazil where the comparative study was done is far better suited to the foraging habits of the Africanized honeybees than are most areas of the United States.

21. The public is well aware that high blood cholesterol levels raise the risk of stroke caused by blood clots. But a recent report concludes that people with low blood cholesterol levels are at increased risk of the other lethal type of stroke—cerebral hemorrhage, caused when a brain artery bursts. The report suggests that because blood cholesterol plays a vital role in maintaining cell membranes, low blood cholesterol weakens artery walls, making them prone to rupture. The conclusion thus supports a long-standing contention by Japanese researchers that Western diets better protect against cerebral hemorrhage than do non-Western diets.

The argument is based on which one of the following assumptions?

(A) Western diets are healthier than non-Western diets.
(B) Western diets result in higher blood cholesterol levels than do non-Western diets.
(C) High blood cholesterol levels preclude the weakening of artery walls.
(D) Cerebral hemorrhages are more dangerous than strokes caused by blood clots.
(E) People who have low blood pressure are at increased risk of cerebral hemorrhage.

GO ON TO THE NEXT PAGE.

22. Public reports by national commissions, governors' conferences, and leadership groups have stressed the great need for better understanding of international affairs by the citizenry. If the country is to remain a leading nation in an era of international competitiveness, the need is undeniable. If there is such a need for the citizenry to have a better understanding of international affairs, then all of our new teachers must be prepared to teach their subject matter with an international orientation.

If all of the statements in the passage are true, which one of the following must also be true?

(A) If the country is to remain a leading nation in an era of international competitiveness, then new teachers must be prepared to teach their subject matter with an international orientation.

(B) If new teachers are prepared to teach their subject matter with an international orientation, then the country will remain a leading nation in an era of international competitiveness.

(C) If there is better understanding of international affairs by the citizenry, then the country will remain a leading nation in an era of international competitiveness.

(D) If the country is to remain a leading nation in an era of international competitiveness, then there is no need for the citizenry to have a better understanding of international affairs.

(E) Public reports from various groups and commissions have stressed the need for a more international orientation in the education of teachers.

23. "DNA fingerprinting" is a recently-introduced biochemical procedure that uses a pattern derived from a person's genetic material to match a suspect's genetic material against that of a specimen from a crime scene. Proponents have claimed astronomically high odds against obtaining a match by chance alone. These odds are based on an assumption that there is independence between the different characteristics represented by a single pattern.

Which one of the following, if true, casts the most doubt on the claim of the proponents of DNA fingerprinting?

(A) The large amount of genetic material that people share with all other people and with other animals is not included in the DNA fingerprinting procedure.

(B) There is a generally accepted theoretical basis for interpreting the patterns produced by the procedure.

(C) In the whole population there are various different subgroups, within each of which certain sets of genetic characteristics are shared.

(D) The skill required of laboratory technicians performing the DNA fingerprinting procedure is not extraordinary.

(E) In the investigation of certain genetic diseases, the techniques used in DNA fingerprinting have traced the transmission of the diseases among the living members of very large families.

GO ON TO THE NEXT PAGE.

24. Anthropologists assert that cultures advance only when independence replaces dependence—that is, only when imposition by outsiders is replaced by initiative from within. In other words, the natives of a culture are the only ones who can move that culture forward. Non-natives may provide valuable advice, but any imposition of their views threatens independence and thus progress. If one looks at individual schools as separate cultures, therefore, the key to educational progress is obvious: _____ .

Which one of the following best completes the passage?

(A) individual schools must be independent of outside imposition

(B) some schools require more independence than others, depending on the initiative of their staffs and students

(C) school system officials must tailor their initiatives for change to each individual school in the system

(D) outsiders must be prevented from participation in schools' efforts to advance

(E) the more independent a school is, the more educational progress it will make

25. The public in the United States has in the past been conditioned to support a substantial defense budget by the threat of confrontation with the Eastern bloc. Now that that threat is dissolving, along with the Eastern bloc itself, it is doubtful whether the public can be persuaded to support an adequate defense budget.

Which one of the following indicates a weakness in the position expressed above?

(A) It presupposes that public opinion can be manipulated indefinitely, without the public's becoming aware of that manipulation.

(B) It refers to past and present events that do not have a causal connection with public support of the budget.

(C) It assumes as fact what it seeks to establish by reasoning.

(D) It fails to give any reason for the judgment it reaches.

(E) It hinges on the term "adequate," the precise meaning of which requires reevaluation in the new context.

S T O P

IF YOU FINISH BEFORE TIME IS CALLED, YOU MAY CHECK YOUR WORK ON THIS SECTION ONLY.
DO NOT WORK ON ANY OTHER SECTION IN THE TEST.

SECTION III
Time—35 minutes
28 Questions

Directions: Each passage in this section is followed by a group of questions to be answered on the basis of what is <u>stated</u> or <u>implied</u> in the passage. For some of the questions, more than one of the choices could conceivably answer the question. However, you are to choose the <u>best</u> answer; that is, the response that most accurately and completely answers the question, and blacken the corresponding space on your answer sheet.

Until recently many astronomers believed that asteroids travel about the solar system unaccompanied by satellites. These astronomers assumed this because they considered asteroid-
(5) satellite systems inherently unstable. Theoreticians could have told them otherwise: even minuscule bodies in the solar system can theoretically have satellites, as long as everything is in proper scale. If a bowling ball were orbiting about the Sun in the
(10) asteroid belt, it could have a pebble orbiting it as far away as a few hundred radii (or about 50 meters) without losing the pebble to the Sun's gravitational pull.

Observations now suggest that asteroid satellites
(15) may exist not only in theory but also in reality. Several astronomers have noticed, while watching asteroids pass briefly in front of stars, that something besides the known asteroid sometimes blocks out the star as well. Is that something a satellite?
(20) The most convincing such report concerns the asteroid Herculina, which was due to pass in front of a star in 1978. Astronomers waiting for the predicted event found not just one occultation, or eclipse, of the star, but two distinct drops in brightness. One was
(25) the predicted occultation, exactly on time. The other, lasting about five seconds, preceded the predicted event by about two minutes. The presence of a secondary body near Herculina thus seemed strongly indicated. To cause the secondary occultation, an
(30) unseen satellite would have to be about 45 kilometers in diameter, a quarter of the size of Herculina, and at a distance of 990 kilometers from the asteroid at the time. These values are within theoretical bounds, and such an asteroid-satellite pair could be stable.
(35) With the Herculina event, apparent secondary occultations became "respectable"—and more commonly reported. In fact, so common did reports of secondary events become that they are now simply too numerous for all of them to be accurate. Even if
(40) every asteroid has as many satellites as can be fitted around it without an undue number of collisions, only one in every hundred primary occultations would be accompanied by a secondary event (one in every thousand if asteroidal satellite systems resembled
(45) those of the planets).

Yet even astronomers who find the case for asteroid satellites unconvincing at present say they would change their minds if a photoelectric record were made of a well-behaved secondary event. By
(50) "well-behaved" they mean that during occultation

the observed brightness must drop sharply as the star winks out and must rise sharply as it reappears from behind the obstructing object, but the brightness during the secondary occultation must drop to that of
(55) the asteroid, no higher and no lower. This would make it extremely unlikely that an airplane or a glitch in the instruments was masquerading as an occulting body.

1. Which one of the following best expresses the main idea of the passage?

   (A) The observation of Herculina represented the crucial event that astronomical observers and theoreticians had been waiting for to establish a convincing case for the stability of asteroid-satellite systems.
   (B) Although astronomers long believed that observation supports the existence of stable asteroid-satellite systems, numerous recent reports have increased skepticism on this issue in astronomy.
   (C) Theoreticians' views on the stability of asteroid-satellite systems may be revised in the light of reports like those about Herculina.
   (D) Astronomers continue to consider it respectable to doubt the stability of asteroid-satellite systems, but new theoretical developments may change their views.
   (E) The Herculina event suggests that theoreticians' views about asteroid-satellite systems may be correct, and astronomers agree about the kind of evidence needed to clearly resolve the issue.

2. Which one of the following is mentioned in the passage as providing evidence that Herculina has a satellite?

   (A) the diameter of a body directly observed near Herculina
   (B) the distance between Herculina and the planet nearest to it
   (C) the shortest possible time in which satellites of Herculina, if any, could complete a single orbit
   (D) the occultation that occurred shortly before the predicted occultation by Herculina
   (E) the precise extent to which observed brightness dropped during the occultation by Herculina

GO ON TO THE NEXT PAGE.

3. According to the passage, the attitude of astronomers toward asteroid satellites since the Herculina event can best be described as

   (A) open-mindedness combined with a concern for rigorous standards of proof

   (B) contempt for and impatience with the position held by theoreticians

   (C) bemusement at a chaotic mix of theory, inadequate or spurious data, and calls for scientific rigor

   (D) hardheaded skepticism, implying rejection of all data not recorded automatically by state-of-the-art instruments

   (E) admiration for the methodical process by which science progresses from initial hypothesis to incontrovertible proof

4. The author implies that which one of the following was true prior to reports of the Herculina event?

   (A) Since no good theoretical model existed, all claims that reports of secondary occultations were common were disputed.

   (B) Some of the reported observations of secondary occultations were actually observations of collisions of satellites with one another.

   (C) If there were observations of phenomena exactly like the phenomena now labeled secondary occultations, astronomers were less likely then to have reported such observations.

   (D) The prevailing standards concerning what to classify as a well-behaved secondary event were less stringent than they are now.

   (E) Astronomers were eager to publish their observations of occultations of stars by satellites of asteroids.

5. The information presented in the passage implies which one of the following about the frequency of reports of secondary occultations after the Herculina event?

   (A) The percentage of reports of primary occultations that also included reports of secondary occultations increased tenfold compared to the time before the Herculina event.

   (B) Primary occultations by asteroids were reported to have been accompanied by secondary occultations in about one out of every thousand cases.

   (C) The absolute number of reports of secondary occultations increased tenfold compared to the time before the Herculina event.

   (D) Primary occultations by asteroids were reported to have been accompanied by secondary occultations in more than one out of every hundred cases.

   (E) In more than one out of every hundred cases, primary occultations were reported to have been accompanied by more than one secondary occultation.

6. The primary purpose of the passage is to

   (A) cast doubt on existing reports of secondary occultations of stars

   (B) describe experimental efforts by astronomers to separate theoretically believable observations of satellites of asteroids from spurious ones

   (C) review the development of ideas among astronomers about whether or not satellites of asteroids exist

   (D) bring a theoretician's perspective to bear on an incomplete discussion of satellites of asteroids

   (E) illustrate the limits of reasonable speculation concerning the occultation of stars

7. The passage suggests that which one of the following would most help to resolve the question of whether asteroids have satellites?

   (A) a review of pre-1978 reports of secondary occultations

   (B) an improved theoretical model of stable satellite systems

   (C) a photoelectric record of a well-behaved secondary occultation

   (D) a more stringent definition of what constitutes a well-behaved secondary occultation

   (E) a powerful telescope that would permit a comparison of ground-based observations with those made from airplanes

GO ON TO THE NEXT PAGE.

Historians attempting to explain how scientific
work was done in the laboratory of the seventeenth-
century chemist and natural philosopher Robert
Boyle must address a fundamental discrepancy
(5) between how such experimentation was actually
performed and the seventeenth-century rhetoric
describing it. Leaders of the new Royal Society of
London in the 1660s insisted that authentic science
depended upon actual experiments performed,
(10) observed, and recorded by the scientists themselves.
Rejecting the traditional contempt for manual
operations, these scientists, all members of the
English upper class, were not to think themselves
demeaned by the mucking about with chemicals,
(15) furnaces, and pumps; rather, the willingness of each
of them to become, as Boyle himself said, a mere
"drudge" and "under-builder" in the search for
God's truth in nature was taken as a sign of their
nobility and Christian piety.
(20) This rhetoric has been so effective that one
modern historian assures us that Boyle himself
actually performed all of the thousand or more
experiments he reported. In fact, due to poor
eyesight, fragile health, and frequent absences from
(25) his laboratory, Boyle turned over much of the labor
of obtaining and recording experimental results to
paid technicians, although published accounts of the
experiments rarely, if ever, acknowledged the
technicians' contributions. Nor was Boyle unique in
(30) relying on technicians without publicly crediting
their work.
Why were the contributions of these technicians
not recognized by their employers? One reason is the
historical tendency, which has persisted into the
(35) twentieth century, to view scientific discovery as
resulting from momentary flashes of individual
insight rather than from extended periods of
cooperative work by individuals with varying levels of
knowledge and skill. Moreover, despite the clamor of
(40) seventeenth-century scientific rhetoric commending a
hands-on approach, science was still overwhelmingly
an activity of the English upper class, and the
traditional contempt that genteel society maintained
for manual labor was pervasive and deeply rooted.
(45) Finally, all of Boyle's technicians were "servants,"
which in seventeenth-century usage meant anyone
who worked for pay. To seventeenth-century
sensibilities, the wage relationship was charged with
political significance. Servants, meaning wage
(50) earners, were excluded from the franchise because
they were perceived as ultimately dependent on their
wages and thus controlled by the will of their
employers. Technicians remained invisible in the
political economy of science for the same reasons
(55) that underlay servants' general political exclusion.
The technicians' contributions, their observations
and judgment, if acknowledged, would not have been
perceived in the larger scientific community as
objective because the technicians were dependent on
(60) the wages paid to them by their employers. Servants
might have made the apparatus work, but their
contributions to the making of scientific knowledge
were largely—and conveniently—ignored by their
employers.

8. Which one of the following best summarizes the main
idea of the passage?

(A) Seventeenth-century scientific experimentation
would have been impossible without the work
of paid laboratory technicians.
(B) Seventeenth-century social conventions
prohibited upper-class laboratory workers
from taking public credit for their work.
(C) Seventeenth-century views of scientific
discovery combined with social class
distinctions to ensure that laboratory
technicians' scientific work was never publicly
acknowledged.
(D) Seventeenth-century scientists were far more
dependent on their laboratory technicians than
are scientists today, yet far less willing to
acknowledge technicians' scientific
contributions.
(E) Seventeenth-century scientists liberated
themselves from the stigma attached to
manual labor by relying heavily on the work of
laboratory technicians.

9. It can be inferred from the passage that the
"seventeenth-century rhetoric" mentioned in line 6
would have more accurately described the
experimentation performed in Boyle's laboratory if
which one of the following were true?

(A) Unlike many seventeenth-century scientists,
Boyle recognized that most scientific
discoveries resulted from the cooperative
efforts of many individuals.
(B) Unlike many seventeenth-century scientists,
Boyle maintained a deeply rooted and
pervasive contempt for manual labor.
(C) Unlike many seventeenth-century scientists,
Boyle was a member of the Royal Society of
London.
(D) Boyle generously acknowledged the
contribution of the technicians who worked in
his laboratory.
(E) Boyle himself performed the actual labor of
obtaining and recording experimental results.

10. According to the author, servants in seventeenth-
century England were excluded from the franchise
because of the belief that

(A) their interests were adequately represented by
their employers
(B) their education was inadequate to make
informed political decisions
(C) the independence of their political judgment
would be compromised by their economic
dependence on their employers
(D) their participation in the elections would be a
polarizing influence on the political process
(E) the manual labor that they performed did not
constitute a contribution to the society that
was sufficient to justify their participation in
elections

GO ON TO THE NEXT PAGE.

11.   According to the author, the Royal Society of London insisted that scientists abandon the

(A)   belief that the primary purpose of scientific discovery was to reveal the divine truth that could be found in nature
(B)   view that scientific knowledge results largely from the insights of a few brilliant individuals rather than from the cooperative efforts of many workers
(C)   seventeenth-century belief that servants should be denied the right to vote because they were dependent on wages paid to them by their employers
(D)   traditional disdain for manual labor that was maintained by most members of the English upper class during the seventeenth century
(E)   idea that the search for scientific truth was a sign of piety

12.   The author implies that which one of the following beliefs was held in both the seventeenth and the twentieth centuries?

(A)   Individual insights rather than cooperative endeavors produce most scientific discoveries.
(B)   How science is practiced is significantly influenced by the political beliefs and assumptions of scientists.
(C)   Scientific research undertaken for pay cannot be considered objective.
(D)   Scientific discovery can reveal divine truth in nature.
(E)   Scientific discovery often relies on the unacknowledged contributions of laboratory technicians.

13.   Which one of the following best describes the organization of the last paragraph?

(A)   Several alternative answers are presented to a question posed in the previous paragraph, and the last is adopted as the most plausible.
(B)   A question regarding the cause of the phenomenon described in the previous paragraph is posed, two possible explanations are rejected, and evidence is provided in support of a third.
(C)   A question regarding the phenomenon described in the previous paragraph is posed, and several incompatible views are presented.
(D)   A question regarding the cause of the phenomenon described in the previous paragraph is posed, and several contributing factors are then discussed.
(E)   Several possible answers to a question are evaluated in light of recent discoveries cited earlier in the passage.

14.   The author's discussion of the political significance of the "wage relationship" (line 48) serves to

(A)   place the failure of seventeenth-century scientists to acknowledge the contributions of their technicians in the larger context of relations between workers and their employers in seventeenth-century England
(B)   provide evidence in support of the author's more general thesis regarding the relationship of scientific discovery to the economic conditions of societies in which it takes place
(C)   provide evidence in support of the author's explanation of why scientists in seventeenth-century England were reluctant to rely on their technicians for the performance of anything but the most menial tasks
(D)   illustrate political and economic changes in the society of seventeenth-century England that had a profound impact on how scientific research was conducted
(E)   undermine the view that scientific discovery results from individual enterprise rather than from the collective endeavor of many workers

15.   It can be inferred from the passage that "the clamor of seventeenth-century scientific rhetoric" (lines 39–40) refers to

(A)   the claim that scientific discovery results largely from the insights of brilliant individuals working alone
(B)   ridicule of scientists who were members of the English upper class and who were thought to demean themselves by engaging in the manual labor required by their experiments
(C)   criticism of scientists who publicly acknowledged the contributions of their technicians
(D)   assertions by members of the Royal Society of London that scientists themselves should be responsible for obtaining and recording experimental results
(E)   the claim by Boyle and his colleagues that the primary reason for scientific research is to discover evidence of divine truth in the natural world

GO ON TO THE NEXT PAGE.

One type of violation of the antitrust laws is the abuse of monopoly power. Monopoly power is the ability of a firm to raise its prices above the competitive level—that is, above the level that would
(5) exist naturally if several firms had to compete—without driving away so many customers as to make the price increase unprofitable. In order to show that a firm has abused monopoly power, and thereby violated the antitrust laws, two essential
(10) facts must be established. First, a firm must be shown to possess monopoly power, and second, that power must have been used to exclude competition in the monopolized market or related markets.

The price a firm may charge for its product is
(15) constrained by the availability of close substitutes for the product. If a firm attempts to charge a higher price—a supracompetitive price—customers will turn to other firms able to supply substitute products at competitive prices. If a firm provides a large
(20) percentage of the products actually or potentially available, however, customers may find it difficult to buy from alternative suppliers. Consequently, a firm with a large share of the relevant market of substitutable products may be able to raise its price
(25) without losing many customers. For this reason courts often use market share as a rough indicator of monopoly power.

Supracompetitive prices are associated with a loss of consumers' welfare because such prices force some
(30) consumers to buy a less attractive mix of products than they would ordinarily buy. Supracompetitive prices, however, do not themselves constitute an abuse of monopoly power. Antitrust laws do not attempt to counter the mere existence of monopoly
(35) power, or even the use of monopoly power to extract extraordinarily high profits. For example, a firm enjoying economies of scale—that is, low unit production costs due to high volume—does not violate the antitrust laws when it obtains a large
(40) market share by charging prices that are profitable but so low that its smaller rivals cannot survive. If the antitrust laws posed disincentives to the existence and growth of such firms, the laws could impair consumers' welfare. Even if the firm, upon acquiring
(45) monopoly power, chose to raise prices in order to increase profits, it would not be in violation of the antitrust laws.

The antitrust prohibitions focus instead on abuses of monopoly power that exclude competition in the
(50) monopolized market or involve leverage—the use of power in one market to reduce competition in another. One such forbidden practice is a tying arrangement, in which a monopolist conditions the sale of a product in one market on the buyer's
(55) purchase of another product in a different market. For example, a firm enjoying a monopoly in the communications systems market might not sell its products to a customer unless that customer also buys its computer systems, which are competing with
(60) other firms' computer systems.

The focus on the abuse of monopoly power, rather than on monopoly itself, follows from the primary purpose of the antitrust laws: to promote consumers' welfare through assurance of the quality and
(65) quantity of products available to consumers.

16. Which one of the following distinctions between monopoly power and the abuse of monopoly power would the author say underlies the antitrust laws discussed in the passage?

(A) Monopoly power is assessed in terms of market share, whereas abuse of monopoly power is assessed in terms of market control.
(B) Monopoly power is easy to demonstrate, whereas abuse of monopoly power is difficult to demonstrate.
(C) Monopoly power involves only one market, whereas abuse of monopoly power involves at least two or more related markets.
(D) Monopoly power is the ability to charge supracompetitive prices, whereas abuse of monopoly power is the use of that ability.
(E) Monopoly power does not necessarily hurt consumer welfare, whereas abuse of monopoly power does.

17. Would the use of leverage meet the criteria for abuse of monopoly power outlined in the first paragraph?

(A) No, because leverage involves a nonmonopolized market.
(B) No, unless the leverage involves a tying arrangement.
(C) Yes, because leverage is a characteristic of monopoly power.
(D) Yes, unless the firm using leverage is charging competitive prices.
(E) Yes, because leverage is used to eliminate competition in a related market.

GO ON TO THE NEXT PAGE.

18. What is the main purpose of the third paragraph (lines 28–47)?

    (A) to distinguish between supracompetitive prices and supracompetitive profits
    (B) to describe the positive uses of monopoly power
    (C) to introduce the concept of economies of scale
    (D) to distinguish what is not covered by the antitrust laws under discussion from what is covered
    (E) to remind the reader of the issue of consumers' welfare

19. Given only the information in the passage, with which one of the following statements about competition would those responsible for the antitrust laws most likely agree?

    (A) Competition is essential to consumers' welfare.
    (B) There are acceptable and unacceptable ways for firms to reduce their competition.
    (C) The preservation of competition is the principal aim of the antitrust laws.
    (D) Supracompetitive prices lead to reductions in competition.
    (E) Competition is necessary to ensure high-quality products at low prices.

20. Which one of the following sentences would best complete the last paragraph of the passage?

    (A) By limiting consumers' choices, abuse of monopoly power reduces consumers' welfare, but monopoly alone can sometimes actually operate in the consumers' best interests.
    (B) What is needed now is a set of related laws to deal with the negative impacts that monopoly itself has on consumers' ability to purchase products at reasonable cost.
    (C) Over time, the antitrust laws have been very effective in ensuring competition and, consequently, consumers' welfare in the volatile communications and computer systems industries.
    (D) By controlling supracompetitive prices and corresponding supracompetitive profits, the antitrust laws have, indeed, gone a long way toward meeting that objective.
    (E) As noted above, the necessary restraints on monopoly itself have been left to the market, where competitive prices and economies of scale are rewarded through increased market share.

GO ON TO THE NEXT PAGE.

Amsden has divided Navajo weaving into four distinct styles. He argues that three of them can be identified by the type of design used to form horizontal bands: colored stripes, zigzags, or
(5) diamonds. The fourth, or bordered, style he identifies by a distinct border surrounding centrally placed, dominating figures.

Amsden believes that the diamond style appeared after 1869 when, under Anglo influence and
(10) encouragement, the blanket became a rug with larger designs and bolder lines. The bordered style appeared about 1890, and, Amsden argues, it reflects the greatest number of Anglo influences on the newly emerging rug business. The Anglo desire that
(15) anything with graphic designs have a top, bottom, and border is a cultural preference that the Navajo abhorred, as evidenced, he suggests, by the fact that in early bordered specimens strips of color unexpectedly break through the enclosing pattern.

(20) Amsden argues that the bordered rug represents a radical break with previous styles. He asserts that the border changed the artistic problem facing weavers: a blank area suggests the use of isolated figures, while traditional, banded Navajo designs were
(25) continuous and did not use isolated figures. The old patterns alternated horizontal decorative zones in a regular order.

Amsden's view raises several questions. First, what is involved in altering artistic styles? Some
(30) studies suggest that artisans' motor habits and thought processes must be revised when a style changes precipitously. In the evolution of Navajo weaving, however, no radical revisions in the way articles are produced need be assumed. After all, all
(35) weaving subordinates design to the physical limitations created by the process of weaving, which includes creating an edge or border. The habits required to make decorative borders are, therefore, latent and easily brought to the surface.

(40) Second, is the relationship between the banded and bordered styles as simple as Amsden suggests? He assumes that a break in style is a break in psychology. But if style results from constant quests for invention, such stylistic breaks are inevitable.
(45) When a style has exhausted the possibilities inherent in its principles, artists cast about for new, but not necessarily alien, principles. Navajo weaving may have reached this turning point prior to 1890.

Third, is there really a significant stylistic gap?
(50) Two other styles lie between the banded styles and the bordered style. They suggest that disintegration of the bands may have altered visual and motor habits and prepared the way for a border filled with separate units. In the Chief White Antelope blanket,
(55) dated prior to 1865, ten years before the first Anglo trading post on the Navajo reservation, whole and partial diamonds interrupt the flowing design and become separate forms. Parts of diamonds arranged vertically at each side may be seen to anticipate the
(60) border.

21. The author's central thesis is that

(A) the Navajo rejected the stylistic influences of Anglo culture
(B) Navajo weaving cannot be classified by Amsden's categories
(C) the Navajo changed their style of weaving because they sought the challenge of new artistic problems
(D) original motor habits and thought processes limit the extent to which a style can be revised
(E) the causal factors leading to the emergence of the bordered style are not as clear-cut as Amsden suggests

22. It can be inferred from the passage that Amsden views the use of "strips of color" (line 18) in the early bordered style as

(A) a sign of resistance to a change in style
(B) an echo of the diamond style
(C) a feature derived from Anglo culture
(D) an attempt to disintegrate the rigid form of the banded style
(E) a means of differentiating the top of the weaving from the bottom

23. The author's view of Navajo weaving suggests which one of the following?

(A) The appearance of the first trading post on the Navajo reservation coincided with the appearance of the diamond style.
(B) Traces of thought processes and motor habits of one culture can generally be found in the art of another culture occupying the same period and region.
(C) The bordered style may have developed gradually from the banded style as a result of Navajo experiments with design.
(D) The influence of Anglo culture was not the only non-Native American influence on Navajo weaving.
(E) Horizontal and vertical rows of diamond forms were transformed by the Navajos into solid lines to create the bordered style.

24. According to the passage, Navajo weavings made prior to 1890 typically were characterized by all of the following EXCEPT

(A) repetition of forms
(B) overall patterns
(C) horizontal bands
(D) isolated figures
(E) use of color

GO ON TO THE NEXT PAGE.

25. The author would most probably agree with which one of the following conclusions about the stylistic development of Navajo weaving?

    (A) The styles of Navajo weaving changed in response to changes in Navajo motor habits and thought processes.
    (B) The zigzag style was the result of stylistic influences from Anglo culture.
    (C) Navajo weaving used isolated figures in the beginning, but combined naturalistic and abstract designs in later styles.
    (D) Navajo weaving changed gradually from a style in which the entire surface was covered by horizontal bands to one in which central figures dominated the surface.
    (E) The styles of Navajo weaving always contained some type of isolated figure.

26. The author suggests that Amsden's claim that borders in Navajo weaving were inspired by Anglo culture could be

    (A) conceived as a response to imagined correspondences between Anglo and Navajo art
    (B) biased by Amsden's feelings about Anglo culture
    (C) a result of Amsden's failing to take into account certain aspects of Navajo weaving
    (D) based on a limited number of specimens of the styles of Navajo weaving
    (E) based on a confusion between the stylistic features of the zigzag and diamond styles

27. The author most probably mentions the Chief White Antelope blanket in order to

    (A) establish the direct influence of Anglo culture on the bordered style
    (B) cast doubts on the claim that the bordered style arose primarily from Anglo influence
    (C) cite an example of a blanket with a central design and no border
    (D) suggest that the Anglo influence produced significant changes in the two earliest styles of Navajo weaving
    (E) illustrate how the Navajo had exhausted the stylistic possibilities of the diamond style

28. The passage is primarily concerned with

    (A) comparing and contrasting different styles
    (B) questioning a view of how a style came into being
    (C) proposing alternate methods of investigating the evolution of styles
    (D) discussing the influence of one culture on another
    (E) analyzing the effect of the interaction between two different cultures

S T O P

IF YOU FINISH BEFORE TIME IS CALLED, YOU MAY CHECK YOUR WORK ON THIS SECTION ONLY.
DO NOT WORK ON ANY OTHER SECTION IN THE TEST.

SECTION IV

Time—35 minutes

24 Questions

Directions: The questions in this section are based on the reasoning contained in brief statements or passages. For some questions, more than one of the choices could conceivably answer the question. However, you are to choose the best answer; that is, the response that most accurately and completely answers the question. You should not make assumptions that are by commonsense standards implausible, superfluous, or incompatible with the passage. After you have chosen the best answer, blacken the corresponding space on your answer sheet.

1. The translator of poetry must realize that word-for-word equivalents do not exist across languages, any more than piano sounds exist in the violin. The violin can, however, play recognizably the same music as the piano, but only if the violinist is guided by the nature and possibilities of the violin as well as by the original composition.

   As applied to the act of translating poetry from one language into another, the analogy above can best be understood as saying that

   (A) poetry cannot be effectively translated because, unlike music, it is composed of words with specific meanings
   (B) some languages are inherently more musical and more suitable to poetic composition than others
   (C) the translator should be primarily concerned with reproducing the rhythms and sound patterns of the original, not with transcribing its meaning exactly
   (D) the translator must observe the spirit of the original and also the qualities of expression that characterize the language into which the original is translated
   (E) poetry is easier to translate if it focuses on philosophical insights or natural descriptions rather than on subjective impressions

2. Behind the hope that computers can replace teachers is the idea that the student's understanding of the subject being taught consists in knowing facts and rules, the job of a teacher being to make the facts and rules explicit and convey them to the student, either by practice drills or by coaching. If that were indeed the way the mind works, the teacher could transfer facts and rules to the computer, which would replace the teacher as drillmaster and coach. But since understanding does not consist merely of knowing facts and rules, but of the grasp of the general concepts underlying them, the hope that the computer will eventually replace the teacher is fundamentally misguided.

   Which one of the following, if true, would most seriously undermine the author's conclusion that computers will not eventually be able to replace teachers?

   (A) Computers are as good as teachers at drilling students on facts and rules.
   (B) The job of a teacher is to make students understand the general concepts underlying specific facts and rules.
   (C) It is possible to program computers so that they can teach the understanding of general concepts that underlie specific facts and rules.
   (D) Because they are not subject to human error, computers are better than teachers at conveying facts and rules.
   (E) It is not possible for students to develop an understanding of the concepts underlying facts and rules through practice drills and coaching.

GO ON TO THE NEXT PAGE.

3. If the city council maintains spending at the same level as this year's, it can be expected to levy a sales tax of 2 percent next year. Thus, if the council levies a higher tax, it will be because the council is increasing its expenditures.

Which one of the following exhibits a pattern of reasoning most closely similar to that of the argument above?

(A) If house-building costs are not now rising, builders cannot be expected to increase the prices of houses. Thus, if they decrease the prices of houses, it will be because that action will enable them to sell a greater number of houses.

(B) If shops wish to reduce shoplifting, they should employ more store detectives. Thus, if shops do not, they will suffer reduced profits because of their losses from stolen goods.

(C) If the companies in the state do not increase their workers' wages this year, the prices they charge for their goods can be expected to be much the same as they were last year. Thus, if the companies do increase prices, it will be because they have increased wages.

(D) If airlines wish to make profits this year that are similar to last year's, they should not increase their prices this year. Thus, if they charge more, they should be expected to improve their services.

(E) If newspaper publishers wish to publish good papers, they should employ good journalists. Thus, if they employ poor journalists, it will not be surprising if their circulation falls as a result.

4. The mind and the immune system have been shown to be intimately linked, and scientists are consistently finding that doing good deeds benefits one's immune system. The bone marrow and spleen, which produce the white blood cells needed to fight infection, are both connected by neural pathways to the brain. Recent research has shown that the activity of these white blood cells is stimulated by beneficial chemicals produced by the brain as a result of magnanimous behavior.

The statements above, if true, support the view that

(A) good deeds must be based on unselfish motives

(B) lack of magnanimity is the cause of most serious illnesses

(C) magnanimous behavior can be regulated by the presence or absence of certain chemicals in the brain

(D) magnanimity is beneficial to one's own interests

(E) the number of white blood cells will increase radically if behavior is consistently magnanimous

5. The high cost of production is severely limiting which operas are available to the public. These costs necessitate reliance on large corporate sponsors, who in return demand that only the most famous operas be produced. Determining which operas will be produced should rest only with ticket purchasers at the box office, not with large corporate sponsors. If we reduce production budgets so that operas can be supported exclusively by box-office receipts and donations from individuals, then the public will be able to see less famous operas.

Which one of the following, if true, would weaken the argument?

(A) A few opera ticket purchasers go to the opera for the sake of going to the opera, not to see specific operatic productions.

(B) The reduction of opera production budgets would not reduce the desire of large corporate sponsors to support operas.

(C) Without the support of large corporate sponsors, opera companies could not afford to produce any but the most famous of operas.

(D) Large corporate sponsors will stop supporting opera productions if they are denied control over which operas will be produced.

(E) The combination of individual donations and box-office receipts cannot match the amounts of money obtained through sponsorship by large corporations.

6. When machines are invented and technologies are developed, they alter the range of choices open to us. The clock, for example, made possible the synchronization of human affairs, which resulted in an increase in productivity. At the same time that the clock opened up some avenues, it closed others. It has become harder and harder to live except by the clock, so that now people have no choice in the matter at all.

Which one of the following propositions is best illustrated by the example presented in the passage?

(A) New machines and technologies can enslave as well as liberate us.

(B) People should make a concerted effort to free themselves from the clock.

(C) Some new machines and technologies bring no improvement to our lives.

(D) The increase in productivity was not worth our dependence on the clock.

(E) Most new machines and technologies make our lives more synchronized and productive.

GO ON TO THE NEXT PAGE.

7. To become an expert on a musical instrument, a person must practice. If people practice a musical instrument for three hours each day, they will eventually become experts on that instrument. Therefore, if a person is an expert on a musical instrument, that person must have practiced for at least three hours each day.

Which one of the following most accurately describes a flaw in the reasoning above?

(A) The conclusion fails to take into account that people who practice for three hours every day might not yet have reached a degree of proficiency that everyone would consider expert.
(B) The conclusion fails to take into account that practicing for less than three hours each day may be enough for some people to become experts.
(C) The conclusion fails to take into account that if a person has not practiced for at least three hours a day, the person has not become an expert.
(D) The conclusion fails to take into account that three consecutive hours of daily practice is not recommended by all music teachers.
(E) The conclusion fails to take into account that few people have the spare time necessary to devote three hours daily to practice.

8. On the basis of incontestable proof that car safety seats will greatly reduce the number of serious injuries sustained by children in car accidents, laws have been passed mandating the use of these seats. Unexpectedly, it has since been found that a large number of children who are riding in safety seats continue to receive serious injuries that safety seats were specifically designed to avoid, and in the prevention of which they in fact have proven to be effective.

Which one of the following, if true, could by itself adequately explain the unexpected finding reported in the passage?

(A) Many parents are defying the law by not using safety seats for their children.
(B) Children are more likely to make automobile trips now than they were before the introduction of the safety seat.
(C) The high cost of child safety seats has caused many parents to delay purchasing them.
(D) The car safety seat was not designed to prevent all types of injuries, so it is not surprising that some injuries are sustained.
(E) The protection afforded by child safety seats depends on their being used properly, which many parents fail to do.

9. An easy willingness to tell funny stories or jokes about oneself is the surest mark of supreme self-confidence. This willingness, often not acquired until late in life, is even more revealing than is good-natured acquiescence in having others poke fun at one.

Which one of the following inferences is most supported by the statements above?

(A) A person who lacks self-confidence will enjoy neither telling nor hearing funny stories about himself or herself.
(B) People with high self-confidence do not tell funny stories or jokes about others.
(C) Highly self-confident people tell funny stories and jokes in order to let their audience know that they are self-confident.
(D) Most people would rather tell a funny story or a joke than listen to one being told.
(E) Telling funny stories or jokes about people in their presence is a way of expressing one's respect for them.

GO ON TO THE NEXT PAGE.

Questions 10–11

Nature constantly adjusts the atmospheric carbon level. An increase in the level causes the atmosphere to hold more heat, which causes more water to evaporate from the oceans, which causes increased rain. Rain washes some carbon from the air into the oceans, where it eventually becomes part of the seabed. A decrease in atmospheric carbon causes the atmosphere to hold less heat, which causes decreased evaporation from the oceans, which causes less rain, and thus less carbon is washed into the oceans. Yet some environmentalists worry that burning fossil fuels may raise atmospheric carbon to a dangerous level. It is true that a sustained increase would threaten human life. But the environmentalists should relax—nature will continually adjust the carbon level.

10. Each of the following can be inferred from the information in the passage EXCEPT:

(A) A decrease in the level of atmospheric heat causes a decrease in the amount of carbon that rain washes into the oceans from the air.

(B) An increase in the level of carbon in the atmosphere causes increased evaporation of ocean water.

(C) An increase in the level of atmospheric heat causes increased rainfall.

(D) A decrease in the level of carbon in the atmosphere causes decreased evaporation of ocean water.

(E) A decrease in the level of atmospheric heat causes a decrease in the level of carbon in the atmosphere.

11. Which one of the following, if true, would most weaken the argument in the passage?

(A) Plant life cannot survive without atmospheric carbon.

(B) It is not clear that breathing excess carbon in the atmosphere will have a negative effect on human life.

(C) Carbon is part of the chemical "blanket" that keeps the Earth warm enough to sustain human life.

(D) Breathing by animals releases almost 30 times as much carbon as does the burning of fossil fuels.

(E) The natural adjustment process, which occurs over millions of years, allows wide fluctuations in the carbon level in the short term.

12. The more television children watch, the less competent they are in mathematical knowledge. More than a third of children in the United States watch television for more than five hours a day; in South Korea the figure is only 7 percent. But whereas less than 15 percent of children in the United States understand advanced measurement and geometric concepts, 40 percent of South Korean children are competent in these areas. Therefore, if United States children are to do well in mathematics, they must watch less television.

Which one of the following is an assumption upon which the argument depends?

(A) Children in the United States are less interested in advanced measurement and geometric concepts than are South Korean children.

(B) South Korean children are more disciplined about doing schoolwork than are children in the United States.

(C) Children who want to do well in advanced measurement and geometry will watch less television.

(D) A child's ability in advanced measurement and geometry increases if he or she watches less than one hour of television a day.

(E) The instruction in advanced measurement and geometric concepts available to children in the United States is not substantially worse than that available to South Korean children.

GO ON TO THE NEXT PAGE.

Questions 13–14

The only way that bookstores can profitably sell books at below-market prices is to get the books at a discount from publishers. Unless bookstores generate a high sales volume, however, they cannot get discounts from publishers. To generate such volume, bookstores must either cater to mass tastes or have exclusive access to a large specialized market, such as medical textbooks, or both.

13. Which one of the following can be properly inferred from the passage?

(A) If a bookstore receives discounts from publishers, it will profitably sell books at below-market prices.

(B) A bookstore that caters to mass tastes or has exclusive access to a large specialized market will have a high sales volume.

(C) A bookstore that profitably sells books at below-market prices gets discounts from publishers.

(D) A bookstore that does not sell books at below-market prices does not get discounts from publishers.

(E) A bookstore that not only caters to mass tastes but also has exclusive access to a large specialized market cannot profitably sell books at below-market prices.

14. If all the statements in the passage are true and if it is also true that a bookstore does not cater to mass tastes, which one of the following CANNOT be true?

(A) The bookstore profitably sells some of its books at below-market prices.

(B) The bookstore does not profitably sell any of its books at below-market prices.

(C) Either the bookstore has exclusive access to a large specialized market or else it does not get a discount from any publishers.

(D) The bookstore does not have exclusive access to a large specialized market but profitably sells some of its books at below-market prices.

(E) The bookstore does not have exclusive access to a large specialized market, nor does it get a discount from any publishers.

15. Extinction is the way of nature. Scientists estimate that over half of the species that have ever come into existence on this planet were already extinct before humans developed even the most primitive of tools. This constant natural process of species emergence and extinction, however, is ignored by those who wish to trace the blame for more recent extinctions to humanity's use of technology, with its consequent effects on the environment. These people must be made to understand that the species that have become extinct in modern times would have become extinct by now even if humans had never acquired technology.

Which one of the following identifies a reasoning error in the passage?

(A) The author mistakenly assumes that technology has not caused any harm to the environment.

(B) The author ignores the fact that some species that are not yet extinct are in danger of extinction.

(C) The author fails to consider that there are probably species in existence that have not yet been identified and studied by scientists.

(D) The author cites scientists who support the theory that over half of all species that ever existed have become extinct, but fails to mention any scientists who do not support that theory.

(E) The author provides no specific evidence that the species that have become extinct in modern times are the same species that would have become extinct in the absence of human technology.

GO ON TO THE NEXT PAGE.

16. The public is aware of the possibility of biases in the mass media and distrusts the media as too powerful. The body of information against which the public evaluates the plausibility of each new media report comes, however, from what the public has heard of through the mass media.

If the view above is correct, it provides a reason for accepting which one of the following conclusions?

(A) If there is a pervasive bias in the presentation of news by the mass media, it would be hard for the public to discern that bias.
(B) The mass media tailor their reports to conform to a specific political agenda.
(C) The biases that news media impose on reporting tend not to be conscious distortions but rather part of a sense they share about what is interesting and believable.
(D) News reporters and their public hold largely the same views about what is most important in society, because news reporters come out of that society.
(E) When a news event occurs that contradicts a stereotype formerly incorporated into reporting by the mass media, the public is predisposed to believe reports of the event.

17. In a bureaucracy, all decisions are arrived at by a process that involves many people. There is no one person who has the authority to decide whether a project will proceed or not. As a consequence, in bureaucracies, risky projects are never undertaken.

The conclusion follows logically from the premises if which one of the following is assumed?

(A) All projects in a bureaucracy require risk.
(B) Decisive individuals choose not to work in a bureaucracy.
(C) An individual who has decision-making power will take risks.
(D) The only risky projects undertaken are those for which a single individual has decision-making power.
(E) People sometimes take risks as individuals that they would not take as part of a group.

18. "Physicalists" expect that ultimately all mental functions will be explainable in neurobiological terms. Achieving this goal requires knowledge of neurons and their basic functions, a knowledge of how neurons interact, and a delineation of the psychological faculties to be explained. At present, there is a substantial amount of fundamental knowledge about the basic functions of neurons, and the scope and character of such psychological capacities as visual perception and memory are well understood. Thus, as the physicalists claim, mental functions are bound to receive explanations in neurobiological terms in the near future.

Which one of the following indicates an error in the reasoning in the passage?

(A) The conclusion contradicts the claim of the physicalists.
(B) The passage fails to describe exactly what is currently known about the basic functions of neurons.
(C) The word "neurobiological" is used as though it had the same meaning as the word "mental."
(D) The argument does not indicate whether it would be useful to explain mental functions in neurobiological terms.
(E) The passage does not indicate that any knowledge has been achieved about how neurons interact.

19. Because a large disparity in pay between the public and private sectors has developed in recent years, many experienced and extremely capable government administrators have quit their posts and taken positions in private-sector management. Government will be able to recapture these capable administrators by raising salaries to a level comparable to those of the private sector. In that way, the functioning of public agencies will be improved.

The position taken above presupposes which one of the following?

(A) Experience gained from private-sector management will be very valuable in government administration.
(B) The most important factor determining how well government agencies function is the amount of experience the administrators have.
(C) Unless government action is taken, the disparity in pay between government administration and private-sector management will continue to increase.
(D) People who moved from jobs in government administration to private-sector management would choose to change careers again.
(E) If the disparity in pay between government administration and private-sector management increases, administrators will move to the public sector in large numbers.

20. Politician: Homelessness is a serious social problem, but further government spending to provide low-income housing is not the cure for homelessness. The most cursory glance at the real-estate section of any major newspaper is enough to show that there is no lack of housing units available to rent. So the frequent claim that people are homeless because of a lack of available housing is wrong.

That homelessness is a serious social problem figures in the argument in which one of the following ways?

(A) It suggests an alternative perspective to the one adopted in the argument.
(B) It sets out a problem the argument is designed to resolve.
(C) It is compatible either with accepting the conclusion or with denying it.
(D) It summarizes a position the argument as a whole is directed toward discrediting.
(E) It is required in order to establish the conclusion.

21. Leona: If the average consumption of eggs in the United States were cut in half, an estimated 5,000 lives might be saved each year.

Thomas: How can that be? That would mean that if people adopt this single change in diet for ten years, the population ten years from now will be greater by 50,000 people than it otherwise would have been.

Which one of the following is a statement that Leona could offer Thomas to clarify her own claim and to address the point he has made?

(A) It is possible for the population to grow by 5,000 people for every year if the base year chosen for purposes of comparison is one with unusually low population growth.
(B) It is accurate to say that 5,000 lives have been saved as long as 5,000 people who would have died in a given year as a result of not changing their diet, did not do so—even if they died for some other reason.
(C) If egg consumption were reduced by more than half, the estimated number of lives saved each year could be even more than 5,000.
(D) The actual rate of population growth depends not only on the birth rate, but also on changes in life expectancy.
(E) For the average consumption of eggs to be cut by half, many individual consumers would have to cut their own consumption by much more than half.

22. The United States Food and Drug Administration (FDA) regulates the introduction of new therapeutic agents into the marketplace. Consequently, it plays a critical role in improving health care in the United States. While it is those in the academic and government research communities who engage in the long process of initial discovery and clinical testing of new therapeutic agents, it is the FDA's role and responsibility to facilitate the transfer of new discoveries from the laboratory to the marketplace. Only after the transfer can important new therapies help patients.

Which one of the following statements can be inferred from the passage?

(A) The FDA is responsible for ensuring that any therapeutic agent that is marketed is then regulated.
(B) Before new therapeutic agents reach the marketplace they do not help patients.
(C) The research community is responsible for the excessively long testing period for new drugs, not the FDA.
(D) The FDA should work more closely with researchers to ensure that the quality of therapeutic agents is maintained.
(E) If a new medical discovery has been transferred from the laboratory to the marketplace, it will help patients.

GO ON TO THE NEXT PAGE.

23. In a new police program, automobile owners in some neighborhoods whose cars are not normally driven between 1 A.M. and 5 A.M. can display a special decal in the cars' windows and authorize police to stop the cars during those hours to check the drivers' licenses. The theft rate for cars bearing such decals is much lower than had been usual for cars in those neighborhoods.

If it is concluded from the statements above that automobile theft has been reduced by the program, which one of the following would it be most important to answer in evaluating that conclusion?

(A) Are owners who are cautious enough to join the program taking other special measures to protect their cars against theft?
(B) In how many neighborhoods is the police program operating?
(C) Are cars in neighborhoods that are actively participating in the program sometimes stolen during daylight hours?
(D) Will owners who have placed decals on their cars' windows but who find it necessary to drive between 1 A.M. and 5 A.M. be harassed by police?
(E) Are the neighborhoods in which the program has been put into effect a representative cross section of neighborhoods with respect to the types of automobiles owned by residents?

24. It has been claimed that an action is morally good only if it benefits another person and was performed with that intention; whereas an action that harms another person is morally bad either if such harm was intended or if reasonable forethought would have shown that the action was likely to cause harm.

Which one of the following judgments most closely conforms to the principle cited above?

(A) Pamela wrote a letter attempting to cause trouble between Edward and his friend; this action of Pamela's was morally bad, even though the letter, in fact, had an effect directly opposite from the one intended.
(B) In order to secure a promotion, Jeffrey devoted his own time to resolving a backlog of medical benefits claims; Jeffrey's action was morally good since it alone enabled Sara's claim to be processed in time for her to receive much-needed treatment.
(C) Intending to help her elderly neighbor by clearing his walkway after a snowstorm, Teresa inadvertently left ice on his steps; because of this exposed ice, her neighbor had a bad fall, thus showing that morally good actions can have bad consequences.
(D) Marilees, asked by a homeless man for food, gave the man her own sandwich; however, because the man tried to talk while he was eating the sandwich, it caused him to choke, and thus Marilees unintentionally performed a morally bad action.
(E) Jonathan agreed to watch his three-year-old niece while she played but, becoming engrossed in conversation, did not see her run into the street where she was hit by a bicycle; even though he intended no harm, Jonathan's action was morally bad.

S T O P

IF YOU FINISH BEFORE TIME IS CALLED, YOU MAY CHECK YOUR WORK ON THIS SECTION ONLY.
DO NOT WORK ON ANY OTHER SECTION IN THE TEST.

Acknowledgment is made to the following for permission to reprint selections that appear in PrepTest III:

From "Economic Goals and Remedies of the AT&T Modified Final Judgment" by Warren G. Lavey and Dennis W. Carlton. *The Georgetown Law Journal*, Volume 71, Notes, 1983. © 1983 by the Georgetown Law Journal Association. Used by permission.

SIGNATURE ——————————————————— | |

DATE

LSAT WRITING SAMPLE TOPIC

Springfield, faced with a 15 percent decrease in the city budget, must cut services in one area. Write an argument in favor of making the cuts in one or the other of the following two areas, keeping in mind two guidelines:

- Springfield wants the cuts to defer spending in a way that will have minimal impact on the quality of services delivered.
- Springfield wants to avoid any negative publicity that could undermine the city government's reputation for effective management.

One way to cope with the budget cuts is to deny funding for the proposed plan to improve Springfield's emergency services. This plan was created after an article in the local newspaper documented problems caused by outdated equipment and one instance in which slow ambulance response may have been responsible for a person's death. A new director with a record of successfully improving services in another town was brought in to take over the emergency services. She designed a plan that calls for hiring three paramedics specially trained with the most advanced equipment. The centerpiece of the plan is the purchase of a computerized dispatching system to improve response time, and a package to train existing staff to use the system.

The alternative is to make cuts in the education budget. One cut would deny teachers their requested salary increases for the coming year. In recent years, Springfield teacher salaries and benefits have risen to compare with the best in the region. The teachers' union has publicly stated that these gains are responsible for the dramatic improvements in student scores on national achievement tests during the last three years. A second cut in the education budget would put off construction of an addition to the high school, at a time when serious overcrowding has already forced the placement of four mobile classroom units behind the existing building. Officials predict that two additional units per year will be needed until the addition is built.

Directions:

1. Use the Answer Key on the next page to check your answers.

2. Use the Scoring Worksheet below to compute your raw score.

3. Use the Score Conversion Chart to convert your raw score into the 120-180 scale.

Scoring Worksheet

1. Enter the number of questions you answered correctly in each section.

Number Correct

SECTION I . . . . . . _____
SECTION II . . . . . _____
SECTION III . . . . . _____
SECTION IV . . . . . _____

2. Enter the sum here: _____
   This is your Raw Score.

Conversion Chart
Form 2LSS13

For Converting Raw Score to the 120-180 LSAT Scaled Score

Reported Score	Raw Score Lowest	Raw Score Highest
180	100	101
179	99	99
178	98	98
177	97	97
176	96	96
175	95	95
174	—*	—*
173	94	94
172	93	93
171	91	92
170	90	90
169	89	89
168	88	88
167	86	87
166	85	85
165	83	84
164	82	82
163	80	81
162	78	79
161	76	77
160	75	75
159	73	74
158	71	72
157	69	70
156	67	68
155	65	66
154	63	64
153	61	62
152	60	60
151	58	59
150	56	57
149	54	55
148	52	53
147	50	51
146	48	49
145	47	47
144	45	46
143	43	44
142	41	42
141	40	40
140	38	39
139	36	37
138	35	35
137	33	34
136	32	32
135	30	31
134	29	29
133	28	28
132	26	27
131	25	25
130	24	24
129	23	23
128	22	22
127	21	21
126	20	20
125	19	19
124	18	18
123	17	17
122	16	16
121	—*	—*
120	0	15

*There is no raw score that will produce this scaled score for this form.

SECTION I

1.	D	8.	C	15.	D	22.	D
2.	B	9.	A	16.	D	23.	B
3.	A	10.	C	17.	E	24.	C
4.	E	11.	A	18.	D		
5.	C	12.	A	19.	A		
6.	A	13.	D	20.	B		
7.	D	14.	A	21.	C		

SECTION II

1.	C	8.	B	15.	D	22.	A
2.	E	9.	D	16.	C	23.	C
3.	D	10.	E	17.	C	24.	A
4.	B	11.	D	18.	C	25.	E
5.	E	12.	D	19.	B		
6.	C	13.	A	20.	C		
7.	A	14.	B	21.	B		

SECTION III

1.	E	8.	C	15.	D	22.	A
2.	D	9.	E	16.	E	23.	C
3.	A	10.	C	17.	E	24.	D
4.	C	11.	D	18.	D	25.	D
5.	D	12.	A	19.	B	26.	C
6.	C	13.	D	20.	A	27.	B
7.	C	14.	A	21.	E	28.	B

SECTION IV

1.	D	8.	E	15.	E	22.	B
2.	C	9.	A	16.	A	23.	A
3.	C	10.	E	17.	D	24.	E
4.	D	11.	E	18.	E		
5.	C	12.	E	19.	D		
6.	A	13.	C	20.	C		
7.	B	14.	D	21.	B		

The Official

LSAT

PrepTest™ VI

The sample test that follows consists of
four sections corresponding to the four
scored sections of the October 1992 LSAT.

October 1992
Form K-2LSS14

INSTRUCTIONS FOR COMPLETING THE BIOGRAPHICAL AREA ARE ON THE BACK COVER OF YOUR TEST BOOKLET.

USE ONLY A NO. 2 OR HB PENCIL TO COMPLETE THIS ANSWER SHEET. DO NOT USE INK.

1 LAST NAME | FIRST NAME | MI

A B C D E F G H I J K L M N O P Q R S T U V W X Y Z

2 DATE OF BIRTH

MONTH	DAY		YEAR	
Jan				
Feb				
Mar	0	0	0	0
Apr	1	1	1	1
May	2	2	2	2
June	3	3	3	3
July		4	4	4
Aug		5	5	5
Sept		6	6	6
Oct		7	7	7
Nov		8	8	8
Dec		9	9	9

3 SOCIAL SECURITY NO.

0 1 2 3 4 5 6 7 8 9

Right Mark:

Wrong Marks:

4 ETHNIC DESCRIPTION

- American Indian/ Alaskan Native
- Asian/Pacific Islander
- Black/African Amer.
- Canadian Aboriginal
- Caucasian/White
- Chicano/Mex. Amer.
- Hispanic
- Puerto Rican
- Other

5 GENDER

- Male
- Female

6 DOMINANT LANGUAGE

- English
- Other

7 ENGLISH FLUENCY

- Yes
- No

8 CENTER NUMBER

0 1 2 3 4 5 6 7 8 9

9 TEST FORM CODE

0 1 2 3 4 5 6 7 8 9

10 TEST BOOK SERIAL NO.

11 TEST FORM

12 TEST DATE

MONTH / DAY / YEAR

13 PLEASE PRINT ALL INFORMATION

LAST NAME FIRST

MAILING ADDRESS

SOCIAL SECURITY/ SOCIAL INSURANCE NO.

LAW SCHOOL ADMISSION TEST

MARK ONE AND ONLY ONE ANSWER TO EACH QUESTION. BE SURE TO FILL IN COMPLETELY THE SPACE FOR YOUR INTENDED ANSWER CHOICE. IF YOU ERASE, DO SO COMPLETELY. MAKE NO STRAY MARKS.

SECTION 1	SECTION 2	SECTION 3	SECTION 4	SECTION 5
1 A B C D E	1 A B C D E	1 A B C D E	1 A B C D E	1 A B C D E
2 A B C D E	2 A B C D E	2 A B C D E	2 A B C D E	2 A B C D E
3 A B C D E	3 A B C D E	3 A B C D E	3 A B C D E	3 A B C D E
4 A B C D E	4 A B C D E	4 A B C D E	4 A B C D E	4 A B C D E
5 A B C D E	5 A B C D E	5 A B C D E	5 A B C D E	5 A B C D E
6 A B C D E	6 A B C D E	6 A B C D E	6 A B C D E	6 A B C D E
7 A B C D E	7 A B C D E	7 A B C D E	7 A B C D E	7 A B C D E
8 A B C D E	8 A B C D E	8 A B C D E	8 A B C D E	8 A B C D E
9 A B C D E	9 A B C D E	9 A B C D E	9 A B C D E	9 A B C D E
10 A B C D E	10 A B C D E	10 A B C D E	10 A B C D E	10 A B C D E
11 A B C D E	11 A B C D E	11 A B C D E	11 A B C D E	11 A B C D E
12 A B C D E	12 A B C D E	12 A B C D E	12 A B C D E	12 A B C D E
13 A B C D E	13 A B C D E	13 A B C D E	13 A B C D E	13 A B C D E
14 A B C D E	14 A B C D E	14 A B C D E	14 A B C D E	14 A B C D E
15 A B C D E	15 A B C D E	15 A B C D E	15 A B C D E	15 A B C D E
16 A B C D E	16 A B C D E	16 A B C D E	16 A B C D E	16 A B C D E
17 A B C D E	17 A B C D E	17 A B C D E	17 A B C D E	17 A B C D E
18 A B C D E	18 A B C D E	18 A B C D E	18 A B C D E	18 A B C D E
19 A B C D E	19 A B C D E	19 A B C D E	19 A B C D E	19 A B C D E
20 A B C D E	20 A B C D E	20 A B C D E	20 A B C D E	20 A B C D E
21 A B C D E	21 A B C D E	21 A B C D E	21 A B C D E	21 A B C D E
22 A B C D E	22 A B C D E	22 A B C D E	22 A B C D E	22 A B C D E
23 A B C D E	23 A B C D E	23 A B C D E	23 A B C D E	23 A B C D E
24 A B C D E	24 A B C D E	24 A B C D E	24 A B C D E	24 A B C D E
25 A B C D E	25 A B C D E	25 A B C D E	25 A B C D E	25 A B C D E
26 A B C D E	26 A B C D E	26 A B C D E	26 A B C D E	26 A B C D E
27 A B C D E	27 A B C D E	27 A B C D E	27 A B C D E	27 A B C D E
28 A B C D E	28 A B C D E	28 A B C D E	28 A B C D E	28 A B C D E
29 A B C D E	29 A B C D E	29 A B C D E	29 A B C D E	29 A B C D E
30 A B C D E	30 A B C D E	30 A B C D E	30 A B C D E	30 A B C D E

NOTE: If you have a new address, you must write Law Services at Box 2000-C, Newtown, PA 18940 or call (215) 968-1001. We cannot guarantee that all address changes will be processed before scores are mailed, so be sure to notify your post office of your forwarding address.

FOR LAW SERVICES USE ONLY
LR
LW
LCS

General Directions for the LSAT Answer Sheet

The actual testing time for this portion of the test will be 2 hours 55 minutes. There are five sections, each with a time limit of 35 minutes. The supervisor will tell you when to begin and end each section. If you finish a section before time is called, you may check your work on that section only; do not turn to any other section of the test book and do not work on any other section either in the test book or on the answer sheet.

There are several different types of questions on the test, and each question type has its own directions. Be sure you understand the directions for each question type before attempting to answer any questions in that section.

Not everyone will finish all the questions in the time allowed. Do not hurry, but work steadily and as quickly as you can without sacrificing accuracy. You are advised to use your time effectively. If a question seems too difficult, go on to the next one and return to the difficult question after completing the section. MARK THE BEST ANSWER YOU CAN FOR EVERY QUESTION. NO DEDUCTIONS WILL BE MADE FOR WRONG ANSWERS. YOUR SCORE WILL BE BASED ONLY ON THE NUMBER OF QUESTIONS YOU ANSWER CORRECTLY.

ALL YOUR ANSWERS MUST BE MARKED ON THE ANSWER SHEET. Answer spaces for each question are lettered to correspond with the letters of the potential answers to each question in the test book. After you have decided which of the answers is correct, blacken the corresponding space on the answer sheet. BE SURE THAT EACH MARK IS BLACK AND COMPLETELY FILLS THE ANSWER SPACE. Give only one answer to each question. If you change an answer, be sure that all previous marks are erased completely. Since the answer sheet is machine scored, incomplete erasures may be interpreted as intended answers. ANSWERS RECORDED IN THE TEST BOOK WILL NOT BE SCORED.

There may be more questions noted on this answer sheet than there are questions in a section. Do not be concerned but be certain that the section and number of the question you are answering matches the answer sheet section and question number. Additional answer spaces in any answer sheet section should be left blank. Begin your next section in the number one answer space for that section.

Score Cancellation

Complete this section only if you are absolutely certain you want to cancel your score. A CANCELLATION REQUEST CANNOT BE RESCINDED. IF YOU ARE AT ALL UNCERTAIN, YOU SHOULD NOT COMPLETE THIS SECTION; INSTEAD, YOU SHOULD USE THE TIME ALLOWED AFTER THE TEST (UP TO 5 DAYS) TO FULLY CONSIDER YOUR DECISION.

To cancel your score from this administration, you must:

A. fill in the ovals here........ ○ ○

B. read the following statement. Then sign your name and enter the date.

I certify that I wish to cancel my test score from this administration. I understand that my request is irreversible and that my score will not be sent to me or to the law schools to which I apply.

_____
Sign your name in full

_____
Date

HOW DID YOU PREPARE FOR THE LSAT?
(Select all that apply.)

Responses to this item are voluntary and will be used for statistical research purposes only.

○ By studying the sample questions in the LSAT/LSDAS Registration and Information Book.
○ By taking the free sample LSAT.
○ By working through The Official LSAT PrepTest(s), PrepBook, Workbooks, or PrepKit.
○ By using a book on how to prepare for the LSAT not published by Law Services.
○ By attending a commercial test preparation or coaching course.
○ By attending a test preparation or coaching course offered through an undergraduate institution.
○ Self study.
○ Other preparation.
○ No preparation.

CERTIFYING STATEMENT

Please write (DO NOT PRINT) the following statement. Sign and date.

I certify that I am the examinee whose name appears on this answer sheet and that I am here to take the LSAT for the sole purpose of being considered for admission to law school. I further certify that I will neither assist nor receive assistance from any other candidate, and I agree not to copy or retain examination questions or to transmit them in any form to any other person.

_____
_____
_____
_____
_____
_____
_____
_____

SIGNATURE: _____ TODAY'S DATE: ___/___/___
MONTH DAY YEAR

SECTION I

Time—35 minutes

27 Questions

<u>Directions:</u> Each passage in this section is followed by a group of questions to be answered on the basis of what is <u>stated</u> or <u>implied</u> in the passage. For some of the questions, more than one of the choices could conceivably answer the question. However, you are to choose the <u>best</u> answer; that is, the response that most accurately and completely answers the question, and blacken the corresponding space on your answer sheet.

The Taft-Hartley Act, passed by the United States Congress in 1947, gave states the power to enact "right-to-work" legislation that prohibits union shop agreements. According to such an
(5) agreement, a labor union negotiates wages and working conditions for all workers in a business, and all workers are required to belong to the union. Since 1947, 20 states have adopted right-to-work laws. Much of the literature concerning
(10) right-to-work laws implies that such legislation has not actually had a significant impact. This point of view, however, has not gone uncriticized. Thomas M. Carroll has proposed that the conclusions drawn by previous researchers are attributable to
(15) their myopic focus on the premise that, unless right-to-work laws significantly reduce union membership within a state, they have no effect. Carroll argues that the right-to-work laws "do matter" in that such laws generate differences in
(20) real wages across states. Specifically, Carroll indicates that while right-to-work laws may not "destroy" unions by reducing the absolute number of unionized workers, they do impede the spread of unions and thereby reduce wages within
(25) right-to-work states. Because the countervailing power of unions is weakened in right-to-work states, manufacturers and their suppliers can act collusively in competitive labor markets, thus lowering wages in the affected industries.
(30) Such a finding has important implications regarding the demographics of employment and wages in right-to-work states. Specifically, if right-to-work laws lower wages by weakening union power, minority workers can be expected to
(35) suffer a relatively greater economic disadvantage in right-to-work states than in union shop states. This is so because, contrary to what was once thought, unions tend to have a significant positive impact on the economic position of minority workers,
(40) especially Black workers, relative to White workers. Most studies concerned with the impact of unionism on the Black worker's economic position relative to the White worker's have concentrated on the changes in Black wages due to union membership. That is,
(45) they have concentrated on union *versus* nonunion wage differentials within certain occupational groups. In a pioneering study, however, Ashenfelter finds that these studies overlook an important fact: although craft unionism increases the
(50) differential between the wages of White workers

and Black workers due to the traditional exclusion of minority workers from unions in the craft sectors of the labor market, strong positive wage gains are made by Black workers within industrial unions.
(55) In fact, Ashenfelter estimates that industrial unionism decreases the differential between the wages of Black workers and White workers by about 3 percent. If state right-to-work laws weaken the economic power of unions to raise wages, Black
(60) workers will experience a disproportionate decline in their relative wage positions. Black workers in right-to-work states would therefore experience a decline in their relative economic positions unless there is strong economic growth in right-to-work
(65) states, creating labor shortages and thereby driving up wages.

1. The reasoning behind the "literature" (line 9), as that reasoning is presented in the passage, is most analogous to the reasoning behind which one of the following situations?

    (A) A law is proposed that benefits many but disadvantages a few; those advocating passage of the law argue that the disadvantages to a few are not so serious that the benefits should be denied to many.

    (B) A new tax on certain categories of consumer items is proposed; those in favor of the tax argue that those affected by the tax are well able to pay it, since the items taxed are luxury items.

    (C) A college sets strict course requirements that every student must complete before graduating; students already enrolled argue that it is unfair for the new requirements to apply to those enrolled before the change.

    (D) The personnel office of a company designs a promotion policy requiring that all promotions become effective on January 1; the managers protest that such a policy means that they cannot respond fast enough to changes in staffing needs.

    (E) A fare increase in a public transportation system does not significantly reduce the number of fares sold; the management of the public transportation system asserts, therefore, that the fare hike has had no negative effects.

GO ON TO THE NEXT PAGE.

2. According to the passage, which one of the following is true of Carroll's study?

   (A) It implies that right-to-work laws have had a negligible effect on workers in right-to-work states.
   (B) It demonstrates that right-to-work laws have significantly decreased union membership from what it once was in right-to-work states.
   (C) It argues that right-to-work laws have affected wages in right-to-work states.
   (D) It supports the findings of most earlier researchers.
   (E) It explains the mechanisms by which collusion between manufacturers and suppliers is accomplished.

3. It can be inferred from the passage that the author believes which one of the following about craft unions?

   (A) Craft unions have been successful in ensuring that the wages of their members remain higher than the wages of nonunion workers in the same occupational groups.
   (B) The number of minority workers joining craft unions has increased sharply in states that have not adopted right-to-work legislation.
   (C) Wages for workers belonging to craft unions have generally risen faster and more steadily than wages for workers belonging to industrial unions.
   (D) The wages of workers belonging to craft unions have not been significantly affected by right-to-work legislation, although the wages of workers belonging to industrial unions have been negatively affected.
   (E) The wages of workers belonging to craft unions are more likely to be driven up in the event of labor shortages than are the wages of workers belonging to industrial unions.

4. Which one of the following best describes the effect industrial unionism has had on the wages of Black workers relative to those of White workers, as that effect is presented in the passage?

   (A) Prior to 1947, industrial unionism had little effect on the wages of Black workers relative to those of White workers; since 1947, it has had a slight positive effect.
   (B) Prior to 1947, industrial unionism had a strong positive effect on the wages of Black workers relative to those of White workers; since 1947, it has had little effect.
   (C) Prior to 1947, industrial unionism had a negative effect on the wages of Black workers relative to those of White workers; since 1947, it has had a significant positive effect.
   (D) Industrial unionism has contributed moderately to an increase in the wage differential between Black workers and White workers.
   (E) Industrial unionism has contributed strongly to a 3 percent decrease in the wage differential between Black workers and White workers.

5. According to the passage, which one of the following could counteract the effects of a decrease in unions' economic power to raise wages in right-to-work states?

   (A) a decrease in the number of union shop agreements
   (B) strong economic growth that creates labor shortages
   (C) a decrease in membership in craft unions
   (D) the merging of large industrial unions
   (E) a decline in the craft sectors of the labor market

6. Which one of the following best describes the passage as a whole?

   (A) an overview of a problem in research methodology and a recommended solution to that problem
   (B) a comparison of two competing theories and a suggestion for reconciling them
   (C) a critique of certain legislation and a proposal for modification of that legislation
   (D) a review of research that challenges the conclusions of earlier researchers
   (E) a presentation of a specific case that confirms the findings of an earlier study

GO ON TO THE NEXT PAGE.

In the late nineteenth century, the need for women physicians in missionary hospitals in Canton, China, led to expanded opportunities for both Western and Chinese women. The presence of (5) Western women as medical missionaries in China was made possible by certain changes within the Western missionary movement. Beginning in the 1870s, increasingly large numbers of women were forming women's foreign mission societies (10) dedicated to the support of women's foreign mission work. Beyond giving the women who organized the societies a formal activity outside their home circles, these organizations enabled an increasing number of single women missionaries (15) (as opposed to women who were part of the more typical husband-wife missionary teams) to work abroad. Before the formation of these women's organizations, mission funds had been collected by ministers and other church leaders, most of whom (20) emphasized local parish work. What money was spent on foreign missions was under the control of exclusively male foreign mission boards whose members were uniformly uneasy about the new idea of sending single women out into the mission field. (25) But as women's groups began raising impressive amounts of money donated specifically in support of single women missionaries, the home churches bowed both to women's changing roles at home and to increasing numbers of single professional (30) missionary women abroad.

Although the idea of employing a woman physician was a daring one for most Western missionaries in China, the advantages of a well-trained Western woman physician could not be (35) ignored by Canton mission hospital administrators. A woman physician could attend women patients without offending any of the accepted conventions of female modesty. Eventually, some of these women were able to found and head separate (40) women's medical institutions, thereby gaining access to professional responsibilities far beyond those available to them at home.

These developments also led to the attainment of valuable training and status by a significant (45) number of Chinese women. The presence of women physicians in Canton mission hospitals led many Chinese women to avail themselves of Western medicine who might otherwise have failed to do so because of their culture's emphasis on physical (50) modesty. In order to provide enough women physicians for these patients, growing numbers of young Chinese women were given instruction in medicine. This enabled them to earn an independent income, something that was then (55) largely unavailable to women within traditional Chinese society. Many women graduates were eventually able to go out on their own into private practice, freeing themselves of dependence upon the mission community.

(60) The most important result of these opportunities

was the establishment of clear evidence of women's abilities and strengths, clear reasons for affording women expanded opportunities, and clear role models for how these abilities and responsibilities (65) might be exercised.

7. Which one of the following statements about Western women missionaries working abroad can be inferred from the passage?

(A) There were very few women involved in foreign missionary work before the 1870s.
(B) Most women working abroad as missionaries before the 1870s were financed by women's foreign mission societies.
(C) Most women employed in mission hospitals abroad before the 1870s were trained as nurses rather than as physicians.
(D) The majority of professional women missionaries working abroad before the 1870s were located in Canton, China.
(E) Most women missionaries working abroad before the 1870s were married to men who were also missionaries.

8. The author mentions that most foreign mission boards were exclusively male most probably in order to

(A) contrast foreign mission boards with the boards of secular organizations sending aid to China
(B) explain the policy of foreign mission boards toward training Chinese women in medicine
(C) justify the preference of foreign mission boards for professionally qualified missionaries
(D) help account for the attitude of foreign mission boards towards sending single women missionaries abroad
(E) differentiate foreign mission boards from boards directing parish work at home

GO ON TO THE NEXT PAGE.

9. Which one of the following best describes the organization of the passage?

(A) A situation is described, conditions that brought about the situation are explained, and results of the situation are enumerated.
(B) An assertion is made, statements supporting and refuting the assertion are examined, and a conclusion is drawn.
(C) An obstacle is identified, a variety of possible ways to overcome the obstacle are presented, and an opinion is ventured.
(D) A predicament is outlined, factors leading up to the predicament are scrutinized, and a tentative resolution of the predicament is recommended.
(E) A development is analyzed, the drawbacks and advantages accompanying the development are contrasted, and an eventual outcome is predicted.

10. Which one of the following, if true, would most undermine the author's analysis of the reason for the increasing number of single women missionaries sent abroad beginning in the 1870s?

(A) The Western church boards that sent the greatest number of single women missionaries abroad had not received any financial support from women's auxiliary groups.
(B) The women who were sent abroad as missionary physicians had been raised in families with a strong history of missionary commitment.
(C) Most of the single missionary women sent abroad were trained as teachers and translators rather than as medical practitioners.
(D) The Western church boards tended to send abroad single missionary women who had previously been active in local parish work.
(E) None of the single missionary women who were sent abroad were active members of foreign mission boards.

11. According to the passage, which one of the following was a factor in the acceptance of Western women as physicians in mission hospitals in Canton, China?

(A) the number of male physicians practicing in that region
(B) the specific women's foreign mission society that supplied the funding
(C) the specific home parishes from which the missionary women came
(D) the cultural conventions of the host society
(E) the relations between the foreign mission boards and the hospital administrators

12. The passage suggests which one of the following about medical practices in late-nineteenth-century Canton, China?

(A) There was great suspicion of non-Chinese medical practices.
(B) Medical care was more often administered in the home than in hospitals.
(C) It was customary for women physicians to donate a portion of their income for the maintenance of their extended family.
(D) It was not customary for female patients to be treated by male physicians.
(E) Young women tended to be afforded as many educational opportunities in medicine as young men were.

GO ON TO THE NEXT PAGE.

In recent years the early music movement, which advocates performing a work as it was performed at the time of its composition, has taken on the character of a crusade, particularly as it has moved
(5) beyond the sphere of medieval and baroque music and into music from the late eighteenth and early nineteenth centuries by composers such as Mozart and Beethoven. Granted, knowledge about the experience of playing old music on now-obsolete
(10) instruments has been of inestimable value to scholars. Nevertheless, the early music approach to performance raises profound and troubling questions.

Early music advocates assume that composers
(15) write only for the instruments available to them, but evidence suggests that composers of Beethoven's stature imagined extraordinarily high and low notes as part of their compositions, even when they recognized that such notes could not be played on
(20) instruments available at the time. In the score of Beethoven's first piano concerto, there is a "wrong" note, a high F-natural where the melody obviously calls for a high F-sharp, but pianos did not have this high an F-sharp when Beethoven composed
(25) the concerto. Because Beethoven once expressed a desire to revise his early works to exploit the extended range of pianos that became available to him some years later, it seems likely that he would have played the F-sharp if given the opportunity.
(30) To use a piano exactly contemporary with the work's composition would require playing a note that was probably frustrating for Beethoven himself to have had to play.

In addition, early music advocates often
(35) inadvertently divorce music and its performance from the life of which they were, and are, a part. The discovery that Haydn's and Mozart's symphonies were conducted during their lifetimes by a pianist who played the chords to keep the
(40) orchestra together has given rise to early music recordings in which a piano can be heard obtrusively in the foreground, despite evidence indicating that the orchestral piano was virtually inaudible to audiences at eighteenth-century
(45) concerts and was dropped as musically unnecessary when a better way to beat time was found. And although in the early nineteenth century the first three movements (sections) of Mozart's and Beethoven's symphonies were often played faster,
(50) and the last movement slower, than today, this difference can readily be explained by the fact that at that time audiences applauded at the end of each movement, rather than withholding applause until the end of the entire work. As a result, musicians
(55) were not forced into extra brilliance in the finale in order to generate applause, as they are now. To restore the original tempo of these symphonies represents an irrational denial of the fact that our concepts of musical intensity and excitement have,
(60) quite simply, changed.

13. It can be inferred from the passage that by "a piano exactly contemporary" (line 30) with the composition of Beethoven's first piano concerto, the author means the kind of piano that was

(A) designed to be inaudible to the audience when used by conductors of orchestras
(B) incapable of playing the high F-natural that is in the score of Beethoven's original version of the concerto
(C) unavailable to Mozart and Haydn
(D) incapable of playing the high F-sharp that the melody of the concerto calls for
(E) influential in Beethoven's decision to revise his early compositions

14. Which one of the following best expresses the main idea of the passage?

(A) The early music movement has yet to resolve a number of troubling questions regarding its approach to the performance of music.
(B) The early music movement, while largely successful in its approach to the performance of medieval and baroque music, has yet to justify its use of obsolete instruments in the performance of music by Beethoven and Mozart.
(C) The early music approach to performance often assumes that composers write music that is perfectly tailored to the limitations of the instruments on which it will be performed during their lifetimes.
(D) Although advocates of early music know much about the instruments used to perform music at the time it was composed, they lack information regarding how the style of such performances has changed since such music was written.
(E) The early music movement has not yet fully exploited the knowledge that it has gained from playing music on instruments available at the time such music was composed.

15. In the second paragraph, the author discusses Beethoven's first piano concerto primarily in order to

(A) illustrate how piano music began to change in response to the extended range of pianos that became available during Beethoven's lifetime
(B) illustrate how Beethoven's work failed to anticipate the changes in the design of instruments that were about to be made during his lifetime
(C) suggest that early music advocates commonly perform music using scores that do not reflect revisions made to the music years after it was originally composed
(D) illustrate how composers like Beethoven sometimes composed music that called for notes that could not be played on instruments that were currently available
(E) provide an example of a piano composition that is especially amenable to being played on pianos available at the time the music was composed

16. The author suggests that the final movements of symphonies by Mozart and Beethoven might be played more slowly by today's orchestras if which one of the following were to occur?

   (A) orchestras were to use instruments no more advanced in design than those used by orchestras at the time Mozart and Beethoven composed their symphonies
   (B) audiences were to return to the custom of applauding at the end of each movement of a symphony
   (C) audiences were to reserve their most enthusiastic applause for the most brilliantly played finales
   (D) conductors were to return to the practice of playing the chords on an orchestral piano to keep the orchestra together
   (E) conductors were to conduct the symphonies in the manner in which Beethoven and Mozart had conducted them

17. Which one of the following best describes the organization of the last paragraph?

   (A) A generalization is made, evidence undermining it is presented, and a conclusion rejecting it is then drawn.
   (B) A criticism is stated and then elaborated with two supporting examples.
   (C) An assumption is identified and then evidence undermining its validity is presented.
   (D) An assertion is made and evidence frequently provided in support of it is then critically evaluated.
   (E) Two specific cases are presented and then a conclusion regarding their significance is drawn.

18. It can be inferred from the passage that the author's explanation in lines 50-54 would be most weakened if which one of the following were true?

   (A) Musicians who perform in modern orchestras generally receive more extensive training than did their nineteenth-century counterparts.
   (B) Breaks between the movements of symphonies performed during the early nineteenth century often lasted longer than they do today because nineteenth-century musicians needed to retune their instruments between each movement.
   (C) Early nineteenth-century orchestral musicians were generally as concerned with the audience's response to their music as are the musicians who perform today in modern orchestras.
   (D) Early nineteenth-century audiences applauded only perfunctorily after the first three movements of symphonies and conventionally withheld their most enthusiastic applause until the final movement was completed.
   (E) Early nineteenth-century audiences were generally more knowledgeable about music than are their modern counterparts.

19. It can be inferred from the passage that the author would be most likely to agree with which one of the following assertions regarding the early music recordings mentioned in the third paragraph?

   (A) These recordings fail to recognize that the last movements of Haydn's and Mozart's symphonies were often played slower in the eighteenth century than they are played today.
   (B) These recordings betray the influence of baroque musical styles on those early music advocates who have recently turned their attention to the music of Haydn and Mozart.
   (C) By making audible the sound of an orchestral piano that was inaudible in eighteenth-century performances, these recordings attempt to achieve aesthetic integrity at the expense of historical authenticity.
   (D) By making audible the sound of an orchestral piano that was inaudible in eighteenth-century performances, these recordings unwittingly create music that is unlike what eighteenth-century audiences heard.
   (E) These recordings suggest that at least some advocates of early music recognize that concepts of musical intensity and excitement have changed since Haydn and Mozart composed their symphonies.

20. The author suggests that the modern audience's tendency to withhold applause until the end of a symphony's performance is primarily related to which one of the following?

   (A) the replacement of the orchestral piano as a method of keeping the orchestra together
   (B) a gradual increase since the time of Mozart and Beethoven in audiences' expectations regarding the ability of orchestral musicians
   (C) a change since the early nineteenth century in audiences' concepts of musical excitement and intensity
   (D) a more sophisticated appreciation of the structural integrity of the symphony as a piece of music
   (E) the tendency of orchestral musicians to employ their most brilliant effects in the early movements of symphonies composed by Mozart and Beethoven

GO ON TO THE NEXT PAGE.

Although the United States steel industry faces widely publicized economic problems that have eroded its steel production capacity, not all branches of the industry have been equally affected. The steel (5) industry is not monolithic: it includes integrated producers, minimills, and specialty-steel mills. The integrated producers start with iron ore and coal and produce a wide assortment of shaped steels. The minimills reprocess scrap steel into a limited (10) range of low-quality products, such as reinforcing rods for concrete. The specialty-steel mills are similar to minimills in that they tend to be smaller than the integrated producers and are based on scrap, but they manufacture much more expensive (15) products than minimills do and commonly have an active in-house research-and-development effort.

Both minimills and specialty-steel mills have succeeded in avoiding the worst of the economic difficulties that are afflicting integrated steel (20) producers, and some of the mills are quite profitable. Both take advantage of new technology for refining and casting steel, such as continuous casting, as soon as it becomes available. The minimills concentrate on producing a narrow range (25) of products for sale in their immediate geographic area, whereas specialty-steel mills preserve flexibility in their operations in order to fulfill a customer's particular specifications.

Among the factors that constrain the (30) competitiveness of integrated producers are excessive labor, energy, and capital costs, as well as manufacturing inflexibility. Their equipment is old and less automated, and does not incorporate many of the latest refinements in steelmaking technology. (35) (For example, only about half of the United States integrated producers have continuous casters, which combine pouring and rolling into one operation and thus save the cost of separate rolling equipment.) One might conclude that the older, (40) labor-intensive machinery still operating in United States integrated plants is at fault for the poor performance of the United States industry, but this cannot explain why Japanese integrated producers, who produce a higher-quality product using less (45) energy and labor, are also experiencing economic trouble. The fact is that the common technological denominator of integrated producers is an inherently inefficient process that is still rooted in the nineteenth century.

(50) Integrated producers have been unable to compete successfully with minimills because the minimills, like specialty-steel mills, have dispensed almost entirely with the archaic energy- and capital-intensive front end of integrated steelmaking: (55) the iron-smelting process, including the mining and preparation of the raw materials and the blast-furnace operation. In addition, minimills have found a profitable way to market steel products: as indicated above, they sell their finished products (60) locally, thereby reducing transportation costs, and

concentrate on a limited range of shapes and sizes within a narrow group of products that can be manufactured economically. For these reasons, minimills have been able to avoid the economic (65) decline affecting integrated steel producers.

21. Which one of the following best expresses the main idea of the passage?

(A) United States steel producers face economic problems that are shared by producers in other nations.
(B) Minimills are the most successful steel producers because they best meet market demands for cheap steel.
(C) Minimills and specialty-steel mills are more economically competitive than integrated producers because they use new technology and avoid the costs of the iron-smelting process.
(D) United States steel producers are experiencing an economic decline that can be traced back to the nineteenth century.
(E) New steelmaking technologies such as continuous casting will replace blast-furnace operations to reverse the decline in United States steel production.

22. The author mentions all of the following as features of minimills EXCEPT

(A) flexibility in their operations
(B) local sale of their products
(C) avoidance of mining operations
(D) use of new steel-refining technology
(E) a limited range of low-quality products

23. The author of the passage refers to "Japanese integrated producers" (line 43) primarily in order to support the view that

(A) different economic difficulties face the steel industries of different nations
(B) not all integrated producers share a common technological denominator
(C) labor-intensive machinery cannot be blamed for the economic condition of United States integrated steel producers
(D) modern steelmaking technology is generally labor- and energy-efficient
(E) labor-intensive machinery is an economic burden on United States integrated steel producers

GO ON TO THE NEXT PAGE.

24. Which one of the following best describes the organization of the third paragraph?

    (A) A hypothesis is proposed and supported; then an opposing view is presented and criticized.
    (B) A debate is described and illustrated; then a contrast is made and the debate is resolved.
    (C) A dilemma is described and cited as evidence for a broader criticism.
    (D) A proposition is stated and argued, then rejected in favor of a more general statement, which is supported with additional evidence.
    (E) General statements are made and details given; then an explanation is proposed and rejected, and an alternative is offered.

25. It can be inferred from the passage that United States specialty-steel mills generally differ from integrated steel producers in that the specialty-steel mills

    (A) sell products in a restricted geographical area
    (B) share the economic troubles of the minimills
    (C) resemble specialty-steel mills found in Japan
    (D) concentrate on producing a narrow range of products
    (E) do not operate blast furnaces

26. Each of the following describes an industry facing a problem also experienced by United States integrated steel producers EXCEPT

    (A) a paper-manufacturing company that experiences difficulty in obtaining enough timber and other raw materials to meet its orders
    (B) a food-canning plant whose canning machines must constantly be tended by human operators
    (C) a textile firm that spends heavily on capital equipment and energy to process raw cotton before it is turned into fabric
    (D) a window-glass manufacturer that is unable to produce quickly different varieties of glass with special features required by certain customers
    (E) a leather-goods company whose hand-operated cutting and stitching machines were manufactured in Italy in the 1920s

27. Which one of the following, if true, would best serve as supporting evidence for the author's explanation of the economic condition of integrated steel producers?

    (A) Those nations that derive a larger percentage of their annual steel production from minimills than the United States does also have a smaller per capita trade deficit.
    (B) Many integrated steel producers are as adept as the specialty-steel mills at producing high-quality products to meet customer specifications.
    (C) Integrated steel producers in the United States are rapidly adopting the production methods of Japanese integrated producers.
    (D) Integrated steel producers in the United States are now attempting to develop a worldwide market by advertising heavily.
    (E) Those nations in which iron-smelting operations are carried out independently of steel production must heavily subsidize those operations in order to make them profitable.

S T O P

IF YOU FINISH BEFORE TIME IS CALLED, YOU MAY CHECK YOUR WORK ON THIS SECTION ONLY.
DO NOT WORK ON ANY OTHER SECTION IN THE TEST.

SECTION II

Time—35 minutes

25 Questions

Directions: The questions in this section are based on the reasoning contained in brief statements or passages. For some questions, more than one of the choices could conceivably answer the question. However, you are to choose the best answer; that is, the response that most accurately and completely answers the question. You should not make assumptions that are by commonsense standards implausible, superfluous, or incompatible with the passage. After you have chosen the best answer, blacken the corresponding space on your answer sheet.

1. A law that is not consistently enforced does not serve its purpose. Law without enforcement is not law; it is merely statute—a promise of law. To institute real law is not merely to declare that such and such behavior is forbidden; it is also to punish those who violate that edict. Furthermore, those who enforce law must punish without favor for their friends or malice for their enemies. To punish only those one dislikes while forgiving others is not to enforce law but to engage in the arbitrary and unjust exercise of power.

   The main point of the passage is that instituting real law consists in

   (A) the exercise of power
   (B) authorizing the enforcement of punishments
   (C) the unbiased punishment of prohibited behavior
   (D) understanding the purpose of law
   (E) clearly defining unacceptable behavior

2. Physiological research has uncovered disturbing evidence linking a number of structural disorders to jogging. Among the ailments seemingly connected with this now-popular sport are spinal disk displacements, stress fractures of the feet and ankles, knee and hip joint deterioration, and tendonitis. Furthermore, these injuries do not occur exclusively among beginning runners—veteran joggers suffer an equal percentage of injuries. What the accumulating data suggest is that the human anatomy is not able to withstand the stresses of jogging.

   Which one of the following is an assumption of the argument?

   (A) The link between jogging and certain structural disorders appears to be a causal one.
   (B) Jogging causes more serious disorders than other sports.
   (C) The jogger's level of experience is a factor determining the likelihood of a jogging injury.
   (D) Some sports are safer for the human body than jogging.
   (E) The human species is not very durable.

3. All students at Pitcombe College were asked to label themselves conservative, liberal, or middle-of-the-road politically. Of the students, 25 percent labeled themselves conservative, 24 percent labeled themselves liberal, and 51 percent labeled themselves middle-of-the-road. When asked about a particular set of issues, however, 77 percent of the students endorsed what is generally regarded as a liberal position.

   If all of the statements above are true, which one of the following must also be true?

   (A) All students who labeled themselves liberal endorsed what is generally regarded as a liberal position on that set of issues.
   (B) More students who labeled themselves middle-of-the-road than students who labeled themselves liberal opposed what is generally regarded as a liberal position on that set of issues.
   (C) The majority of students who labeled themselves middle-of-the-road opposed what is generally regarded as a liberal position on that set of issues.
   (D) Some students who labeled themselves conservative endorsed what is generally regarded as a liberal position on that set of issues.
   (E) Some students who labeled themselves liberal endorsed what is generally regarded as a conservative position on that set of issues.

GO ON TO THE NEXT PAGE.

4. Lenore: It is naive to think that historical explanations can be objective. In evaluating evidence, historians are always influenced by their national, political, and class loyalties.

    Victor: Still, the very fact that cases of biased thinking have been detected and sources of bias identified shows that there are people who can maintain objectivity.

Victor's response does not succeed as a rebuttal of Lenore's argument because his response

(A) displays the same kind of biased thinking as that against which Lenore's argument is directed

(B) does not address the special case of historians who purposely distort evidence in order to promote their own political objectives

(C) fails to provide examples of cases in which biased thinking has been detected and the source of that bias identified

(D) does not consider sources of bias in historical explanation other than those that are due to national, political, and class loyalties.

(E) overlooks the possibility that those who detect and identify bias are themselves biased in some way

5. The museum's night security guard maintains that the thieves who stole the portrait did not enter the museum at any point at or above ground level. Therefore, the thieves must have gained access to the museum from below ground level.

The flawed pattern of reasoning in the argument above is most similar to that in which one of the following?

(A) The rules stipulate the participants in the contest be judged on both form and accuracy. The eventual winner was judged highest in neither category, so there must be a third criterion that judges were free to invoke.

(B) The store's competitors claim that the store, in selling off the shirts at those prices, neither made any profit nor broke even. Consequently, the store's customers must have been able to buy shirts there at less than the store's cost.

(C) If the census is to be believed, the percentage of men who are married is higher than the percentage of women who are married. Thus, the census must show a higher number of men than of women overall.

(D) The product label establishes that this insecticide is safe for both humans and pets. Therefore, the insecticide must also be safe for such wild mammals as deer and rabbits.

(E) As had generally been expected, not all questionnaires were sent in by the official deadline. It follows that plans must have been made for the processing of questionnaires received late.

GO ON TO THE NEXT PAGE.

Questions 6–7

High-technology medicine is driving up the nation's health care costs. Recent advances in cataract surgery illustrate why this is occurring. Cataracts are a major cause of blindness, especially in elderly people. Ten years ago, cataract surgery was painful and not always effective. Thanks to the new technology used in cataract surgery, the operation now restores vision dramatically and is less expensive. These two factors have caused the number of cataract operations performed to increase greatly, which has, in turn, driven up the total amount spent on cataract surgery.

6. Which one of the following can be inferred from the passage?

   (A) Ten years ago, few people had successful cataract surgery.
   (B) In the long run, the advantages of advanced medical technology are likely to be outweighed by the disadvantages.
   (C) The total amount spent on cataract surgery has increased because the increased number of people electing to have the surgery more than offsets the decrease in cost per operation.
   (D) Huge increases in the nation's health care costs are due primarily to increased demand for surgery for older people.
   (E) Ten years ago, cataract surgery was affordable for more people than it was last year.

7. Each of the following, if true, would support a challenge to the author's explanation of the increase in the number of cataract operations EXCEPT:

   (A) The overall population of the nation has increased from what it was ten years ago.
   (B) Any one individual's chance of developing cataracts is greater than it was ten years ago.
   (C) The number of older people has increased during the last ten years.
   (D) Today, health insurance covers cataract surgery for more people than it did ten years ago.
   (E) People who have had unsuccessful cataract surgery are left with more seriously impaired vision than they had before the surgery.

8. Some companies in fields where skilled employees are hard to find make signing an "agreement not to compete" a condition of employment. In such an agreement the employee promises not to go to work for a competing firm for a set period after leaving his or her current employer. Courts are increasingly ruling that these agreements are not binding. Yet paradoxically, for people who signed such agreements when working for competing firms, many firms are unwilling to consider hiring them during the period covered by the agreement.

Which one of the following, if true, most helps to resolve the paradox?

   (A) Many companies will not risk having to become involved in lawsuits, even suits that they expect to have a favorable outcome, because of the associated costs and publicity.
   (B) In some industries, for example the broadcast media, companies' main source of new employees tends to be people who are already employed by competing firms.
   (C) Most companies that require their employees to sign agreements not to compete are aware that these documents are not legally binding.
   (D) Many people who have signed agreements not to compete are unwilling to renege on a promise by going to work for a competing firm.
   (E) Many companies consider their employees' established relationships with clients and other people outside the company to be valuable company assets.

9. Mary Ann: Our country should, above all, be strong. Strength gains the respect of other countries and makes a country admirable.

   Inez: There are many examples in history of countries that were strong but used their strength to commit atrocities. We should judge a country by the morality of its actions, not by its strength. If the actions are morally good, the country is admirable.

Which one of the following is a presupposition that underlies Inez' argument?

   (A) At least one country is admirable.
   (B) Countries cannot be both strong and moral.
   (C) It is possible to assign moral weight to the actions of countries.
   (D) The citizens of any country believe that whatever their country does is good.
   (E) Countries should impose their standards of morality on other countries by whatever means necessary.

10. All of John's friends say they know someone who has smoked 40 cigarettes a day for the past 40 years and yet who is really fit and well. John does not know anyone like that and it is quite certain that he is not unique among his friends in this respect.

If the statements in the passage are true, then which one of the following must also be true?

(A) Smokers often lie about how much they smoke.
(B) People often knowingly exaggerate without intending to lie.
(C) All John's friends know the same lifelong heavy smoker.
(D) Most of John's friends are not telling the truth.
(E) Some of John's friends are not telling the truth.

11. For democracy to survive, it is imperative that the average citizen be able to develop informed opinions about important policy issues. In today's society, this means that citizens must be able to develop informed opinions on many scientific subjects, from ecosystems to defense systems. Yet, as scientific knowledge advances, the average citizen is increasingly unable to absorb enough information to develop informed opinions on many important issues.

Of the following, which one follows logically from the passage?

(A) Scientists have a duty to educate the public.
(B) The survival of democracy is threatened by the advance of scientific knowledge.
(C) Every citizen has a duty to and can become scientifically literate.
(D) The most effective democracy is one that is the most scientifically unsophisticated.
(E) Democracy will survive if there are at least some citizens who are capable of developing informed opinions on important scientific issues.

12. By dating fossils of pollen and beetles, which returned after an Ice Age glacier left an area, it is possible to establish an approximate date when a warmer climate developed. In one glacial area, it appears from the insect record that a warm climate developed immediately after the melting of the glacier. From the pollen record, however, it appears that the warm climate did not develop until long after the glacier disappeared.

Each one of the following, if true, helps to explain the apparent discrepancy EXCEPT:

(A) Cold-weather beetle fossils can be mistaken for those of beetles that live in warm climates.
(B) Warm-weather plants cannot establish themselves as quickly as can beetles in a new environment.
(C) Beetles can survive in a relatively barren postglacial area by scavenging.
(D) Since plants spread unevenly in a new climate, researchers can mistake gaps in the pollen record as evidence of no new overall growth.
(E) Beetles are among the oldest insect species and are much older than many warm-weather plants.

13. Using clean-coal technologies to "repower" existing factories promises ultimately a substantial reduction of polluting emissions, and will affect the full range of pollutants implicated in acid rain. The strategy of using these technologies could cut sulfur dioxide emissions by more than 80 percent and nitrogen oxide emissions by more than 50 percent. The emission of a smaller quantity of nitrogen pollutants would in turn reduce the formation of noxious ozone in the troposphere.

Which one of the following statements is an inference that can be drawn from the information given in the passage?

(A) Sulfur dioxide emissions are the most dangerous pollutants implicated in acid rain.
(B) Noxious ozone is formed in factories by chemical reactions involving sulfur dioxide.
(C) Twenty percent of the present level of sulfur dioxide emissions in the atmosphere is not considered a harmful level.
(D) A substantial reduction of polluting emissions will be achieved by the careful design of new factories.
(E) The choice of technologies in factories could reduce the formation of noxious ozone in the troposphere.

GO ON TO THE NEXT PAGE.

14. Joshua Smith's new novel was criticized by the book editor for *The Daily Standard* as implausible. That criticism, like so many other criticisms from the same source in the past, is completely unwarranted. As anyone who has actually read the novel would agree, each one of the incidents in which Smith's hero gets involved is the kind of incident that could very well have happened to someone or other.

Which one of the following is the most serious error of reasoning in the argument?

(A) It relies on the assumption that a criticism can legitimately be dismissed as unwarranted if it is offered by someone who had previously displayed questionable judgment.

(B) It ignores the fact that people can agree about something even though what they agree about is not the case.

(C) It calls into question the intellectual integrity of the critic in order to avoid having to address the grounds on which the criticism is based.

(D) It takes for granted that a whole story will have a given characteristic if each of its parts has that characteristic.

(E) It attempts to justify its conclusion by citing reasons that most people would find plausible only if they were already convinced that the conclusion was true.

15. J. J. Thomson, the discoverer of the electron and a recipient of the Nobel Prize in physics, trained many physicists, among them seven Nobel Prize winners, 32 fellows of the Royal Society of London, and 83 professors of physics. This shows that the skills needed for creative research can be taught and learned.

Which one of the following is an assumption on which the argument depends?

(A) J. J. Thomson was an internationally known physicist, and scientists came from all over the world to work with him.

(B) All the scientists trained by J. J. Thomson were renowned for their creative scientific research.

(C) At least one of the eminent scientists trained by J. J. Thomson was not a creative researcher before coming to study with him.

(D) Creative research in physics requires research habits not necessary for creative research in other fields.

(E) Scientists who go on to be the most successful researchers often receive their scientific education in classes taught by renowned research scientists.

16. The ancient Romans understood the principles of water power very well, and in some outlying parts of their empire they made extensive and excellent use of water as an energy source. This makes it all the more striking that the Romans made do without water power in regions dominated by large cities.

Which one of the following, if true, contributes most to an explanation of the difference described above in the Romans' use of water power?

(A) The ancient Romans were adept at constructing and maintaining aqueducts that could carry quantities of water sufficient to supply large cities over considerable distances.

(B) In the areas in which water power was not used, water flow in rivers and streams was substantial throughout the year but nevertheless exhibited some seasonal variation.

(C) Water power was relatively vulnerable to sabotage, but any damage could be quickly and inexpensively repaired.

(D) In most areas to which the use of water power was not extended, other, more traditional sources of energy continued to be used.

(E) In heavily populated areas the introduction of water power would have been certain to cause social unrest by depriving large numbers of people of their livelihood.

GO ON TO THE NEXT PAGE.

17. From a book review: The authors blithely claim that there are "three basic ways to store energy: as heat, as electricity, or as kinetic energy." However, I cannot call to mind any effective ways to store energy as electricity, whereas any capable student of physics could readily suggest a few more ways to store energy: chemical, gravitational, nuclear.

The reviewer makes which one of the following criticisms of a claim that appears in the book under review?

(A) There is no reason to consider any particular way to store energy any more basic than any other.

(B) The list given of ways to store energy is possibly inaccurate and certainly not exhaustive.

(C) It is overly limiting to treat basic ways to store energy as a question unrelated to the question of effective ways to use energy.

(D) What needs to be considered is not whether various ways to store energy are basic but whether they are effective.

(E) Except possibly for electricity, all ways to store energy are equally effective and therefore equally basic.

18. There is no mystery as to why figurative painting revived in the late 1970s. People want to look at recognizable images. Sorting out art theories reflected in abstract paintings is no substitute for the sense of empathy that comes from looking at a realistic painting of a figure in a landscape. Perhaps members of the art-viewing public resented abstract art because they felt that its lack of realistic subject matter was a rejection of the viewers and their world.

Which one of the following most accurately expresses the main point of the passage?

(A) Abstract paintings often include shapes or forms that are suggestive of real objects or emotions.

(B) The art-viewing public wished to see traditional subjects treated in a nontraditional manner.

(C) Paintings that depict a recognizable physical world rather than the emotional world of the artist's life require more artistic talent to create.

(D) The general public is unable to understand the theories on which abstract painting is based.

(E) The artistic preferences of the art-viewing public stimulated the revival.

19. Valitania's long-standing practice of paying high salaries to its elected politicians has had a disastrous effect on the level of integrity among politicians in that country. This is because the prospect of earning a high salary is always attractive to anyone whose primary aim in life is to make money, so that inevitably the wrong people must have been attracted into Valitanian politics: people who are more interested in making money than in serving the needs of the nation.

Which one of the following, if true, would weaken the argument?

(A) Many Valitanian candidates for elected office spend some of their own money to finance their campaigns.

(B) Most Valitanian elective offices have four-year terms.

(C) No more people compete for elected office when officeholders are paid well than when they are paid poorly.

(D) Only politicians who rely on their offices for income tend to support policies that advance their own selfish interests.

(E) Most of those who are currently Valitanian politicians could have obtained better-paid work outside politics.

GO ON TO THE NEXT PAGE.

Questions 20–21

Policy Adviser: Freedom of speech is not only a basic human right; it is also the only rational policy for this government to adopt. When ideas are openly aired, good ideas flourish, silly proposals are easily recognized as such, and dangerous ideas can be responded to by rational argument. Nothing is ever gained by forcing citizens to disseminate their thoughts in secret.

20. The policy adviser's method of persuasion, in recommending a policy of free speech to the government, is best described by which one of the following?

(A) a circular justification of the idea of free speech as an idea that flourishes when free speech is allowed
(B) advocating respect for basic rights of citizens for its own sake
(C) a coupling of moral ideals with self-interest
(D) a warning about the difficulty of suppressing the truth
(E) a description of an ideal situation that cannot realistically be achieved

21. Which one of the following, if true, would most strengthen the argument?

(A) Most citizens would tolerate some limits on freedom of speech.
(B) With or without a policy of freedom of speech, governments respond to dangerous ideas irrationally.
(C) Freedom of religion and freedom of assembly are also basic human rights that governments must recognize.
(D) Governments are less likely to be overthrown if they openly adopt a policy allowing freedom of speech.
(E) Great ideas have flourished in societies that repress free speech as often as in those that permit it.

22. The trustees of the Avonbridge summer drama workshop have decided to offer scholarships to the top 10 percent of local applicants and the top 10 percent of nonlocal applicants as judged on the basis of a qualifying audition. They are doing this to ensure that only the applicants with the most highly evaluated auditions are offered scholarships to the program.

Which one of the following points out why the trustees' plan might not be effective in achieving its goal?

(A) The best actors can also apply for admission to another program and then not enroll in the Avonbridge program.
(B) Audition materials that produce good results for one actor may disadvantage another, resulting in inaccurate assessment.
(C) The top 10 percent of local and nonlocal applicants might not need scholarships to the Avonbridge program.
(D) Some of the applicants who are offered scholarships could have less highly evaluated auditions than some of the applicants who are not offered scholarships.
(E) Dividing applicants into local and nonlocal groups is unfair because it favors nonlocal applicants.

23. Book Review: When I read a novel set in a city I know well, I must see that the writer knows the city at least as well as I do if I am to take that writer seriously. If the writer is faking, I know immediately and do not trust that writer. When a novelist demonstrates the required knowledge, I trust the storyteller, so I trust the tale. This trust increases my enjoyment of a good novel. Peter Lee's second novel is set in San Francisco. In this novel, as in his first, Lee passes my test with flying colors.

Which one of the following can be properly inferred from the passage?

(A) The book reviewer enjoys virtually any novel written by a novelist whom she trusts.
(B) If the book reviewer trusts the novelist as a storyteller, the novel in question must be set in a city the book reviewer knows well.
(C) Peter Lee's first novel was set in San Francisco.
(D) The book reviewer does not trust any novel set in a city that she does not know well.
(E) The book reviewer does not believe that she knows San Francisco better than Peter Lee does.

GO ON TO THE NEXT PAGE.

24. Someone's benefiting from having done harm to another person is morally justifiable only if the person who was harmed knew that what was done could cause that harm but consented to its being done anyway.

Which one of the following judgments most closely conforms to the principle above?

(A) Attempting to avoid being kept after school as punishment for breaking a window, Sonia falsely claimed that her brother had broken it; Sonia's action was morally unjustifiable since it resulted in both children being kept after school for something only Sonia had done.

(B) Since Ned would not have won the prize for best model airplane if Penny's brother had not inadvertently damaged her entry while playing with it, Ned is morally unjustified in accepting his prize.

(C) Wesley, a doctor, persuaded Max to take part in a medical experiment in which a new drug was being tested; since Wesley failed to warn Max about the serious side effects of the drug and the drug proved to have no other effects, Wesley was morally unjustified in using the results obtained from Max in his report.

(D) Because Roger's mother suffered severe complications as a result of donating a kidney to him for a lifesaving kidney transplant, it was morally unjustifiable for Roger to receive the transplant, even though his mother, herself a doctor, had been eager for the transplant to be performed.

(E) For James, who was convicted of having defrauded a large number of people out of their savings and wrote a book about his scheme while in prison, to be denied the profits from his book would be morally unjustifiable since he has already been punished for his crime.

25. Certain governments subsidize certain basic agricultural products in order to guarantee an adequate domestic production of them. But subsidies encourage more intensive farming, which eventually leads to soil exhaustion and drastically reduced yields.

The situation above is most nearly similar to which one of the following situations with respect to the relationship between the declared intent of a governmental practice and a circumstance relevant to it?

(A) Certain governments subsidize theaters in order to attract foreign tourists. But tourists rarely choose a destination for the theatrical performances it has to offer.

(B) Certain governments restrict imports in order to keep domestic producers in business. But, since domestic producers do not have to face the full force of foreign competition, some domestic producers are able to earn inordinately high profits.

(C) Certain governments build strong armed forces in order to forestall armed conflict. But in order to maintain the sort of discipline and morale that keeps armed forces strong, those forces must be used in actual combat periodically.

(D) Certain governments reduce taxes on businesses in order to stimulate private investment. But any investment is to some extent a gamble, and new business ventures are not always as successful as their owners hoped.

(E) Certain governments pass traffic laws in order to make travel safer. But the population-driven growth in volumes of traffic often has the effect of making travel less safe despite the passage of new traffic laws.

S T O P

IF YOU FINISH BEFORE TIME IS CALLED, YOU MAY CHECK YOUR WORK ON THIS SECTION ONLY.
DO NOT WORK ON ANY OTHER SECTION IN THE TEST.

SECTION III

Time—35 minutes

26 Questions

Directions: The questions in this section are based on the reasoning contained in brief statements or passages. For some questions, more than one of the choices could conceivably answer the question. However, you are to choose the best answer; that is, the response that most accurately and completely answers the question. You should not make assumptions that are by commonsense standards implausible, superfluous, or incompatible with the passage. After you have chosen the best answer, blacken the corresponding space on your answer sheet.

1. Roses always provide a stunning display of color, but only those flowers that smell sweet are worth growing in a garden. Some roses have no scent.

   Which one the following conclusions can be properly drawn from the passage?

   (A) Some flowers which provide a stunning display of color are not worth growing in a garden.
   (B) All flowers with no scent provide a stunning display of color.
   (C) Some flowers which are worth growing in a garden have no scent.
   (D) Some roses which smell sweet are not worth growing in a garden.
   (E) No sweet-smelling flower is worth growing in a garden unless it provides a stunning display of color.

2. The use of money causes a civilization to decline. That this is true is shown by the way the troubles of Western civilization began with the invention of money. While real money (gold and silver) is bad enough, imitation money (paper money) is a horror. The decline of Western civilization exactly parallels the increasing use of money—both real money and worthless paper money—as a substitute for things of intrinsic value.

   Which one of the following, if true, could contribute most to a refutation of the argument?

   (A) People prefer using money to having a system in which goods are bartered for other goods of equal intrinsic value.
   (B) Eastern cultures have used money, and Eastern civilizations have not declined.
   (C) The use of paper money encourages disregard for the value of work because the money itself has no intrinsic value.
   (D) The rate of exchange between gold and paper money has fluctuated greatly in Western civilization.
   (E) Some employers exchange goods for their employees' services in order to avoid the exchange of money.

3. Fire ants from Brazil now infest the southern United States. Unlike queen fire ants in Brazil, two queens in the United States share a nest. Ants from these nests are more aggressive than those from single-queen nests. By destroying virtually all insects in the nest area, these aggressive ants gain sole access to food sources, and the ant population skyrockets. Since certain predator insects in Brazil limit the fire-ant population there, importing such predator insects into the United States would be of overall benefit to the environment by stopping the increase of the fire-ant population in the United States.

   Each of the following is an assumption made in the argument EXCEPT:

   (A) The imported insects would not prove more damaging to the environment in the United States than are the fire ants themselves.
   (B) The predator insects from Brazil could survive in the ecological environment found in the United States.
   (C) The especially aggressive fire ants from the two-queen nests would not be able to destroy the Brazilian predator insects.
   (D) The predator insects would stop the increase of the ant population before the ants spread to states that are farther north.
   (E) The rate of increase of the fire-ant population would not exceed the rate at which the predator insects could kill the ants.

GO ON TO THE NEXT PAGE.

4. In an attempt to counter complaints that a certain pesticide is potentially hazardous to humans if absorbed into edible plants, the pesticide manufacturer has advertised that "ounce for ounce, the active ingredient in this pesticide is less toxic than the active ingredient in mouthwash."

Which one of the following, if true, indicates a weakness in the manufacturer's argument?

(A) The ounce-for-ounce toxicity of the active ingredient in mouthwash is less than that of most products meant for external use by humans, such as nail polish or other cosmetics.
(B) The quantity of toxins humans ingest by consuming plants treated with the pesticide is, on average, much higher than the quantity of toxins humans ingest by using mouthwash.
(C) The container in which the pesticide is packaged clearly identifies the toxic ingredients and carries warnings about their potential danger to humans.
(D) On average, the toxins present in the pesticide take longer than the toxins present in mouthwash to reach harmful levels in the human body.
(E) Since the government began to regulate the pesticide industry over ten years ago, there has been a growing awareness of the dangers of toxins used in pesticides.

Questions 5-6

Four randomly chosen market research companies each produced population estimates for three middle-sized cities; the estimates of each company were then compared with those of the other companies. Two of the cities had relatively stable populations, and for them estimates of current population and of projected population in five years varied little from company to company. However, for the third city, which was growing rapidly, estimates varied greatly from company to company.

5. The passage provides the most support for which one of the following?

(A) It is more difficult to estimate the population of middle-sized cities than of smaller cities.
(B) Population estimates for rapidly growing cities can be accurate enough to be useful for marketing.
(C) The rate of change in population of rapidly growing cities does not fluctuate.
(D) The market research companies are likely to be equally reliable in estimating the population of stable cities.
(E) Estimates of a city's future population are likely to be more accurate than are estimates of that city's current population.

6. Which one of the following, if true, would best help explain why estimates of the current population of the rapidly growing city varied more than did current population estimates for the two other cities?

(A) Population changes over time are more uniform from one district to another in the rapidly growing city than in the two other cities.
(B) The population of the rapidly growing city is increasing largely as a result of a high birth rate.
(C) The population of the rapidly growing city has a lower average age than the populations of either of the two other cities.
(D) All population estimates of the rapidly growing city were produced first by estimating the current populations of the city's districts and then by adding those estimates.
(E) Whereas the companies used different methods for estimating the current population of the rapidly growing city, the companies used the same method for the two other cities.

GO ON TO THE NEXT PAGE.

7. Head injury is the most serious type of injury sustained in motorcycle accidents. The average cost to taxpayers for medical care for nonhelmeted motorcycle-accident victims is twice that for their helmeted counterparts. Jurisdictions that have enacted motorcycle-helmet laws have reduced the incidence and severity of accident-related head injuries, thereby reducing the cost to taxpayers. Therefore, to achieve similar cost reductions, other jurisdictions should enact motorcycle-helmet laws. For the same reason jurisdictions should also require helmets for horseback riders, since horseback-riding accidents are even more likely to cause serious head injury than motorcycle accidents are.

Which one of the following is an assumption upon which the author's conclusion concerning helmets for horseback riders depends?

(A) Medical care for victims of horseback-riding accidents is a financial drain on tax funds.
(B) The higher rate of serious head injury suffered by victims of horseback-riding accidents is due to the difference in size between horses and motorcycles.
(C) The medical costs associated with treating head injuries are higher than those for other types of injury.
(D) Most fatalities resulting from horseback-riding and motorcycle accidents could have been prevented if the victims had been wearing helmets.
(E) When deciding whether to enact helmet laws for motorcyclists and horseback riders, the jurisdiction's primary concern is the safety of its citizens.

8. The senator has long held to the general principle that no true work of art is obscene, and thus that there is no conflict between the need to encourage free artistic expression and the need to protect the sensibilities of the public from obscenity. When well-known works generally viewed as obscene are cited as possible counterexamples, the senator justifies accepting the principle by saying that if these works really are obscene then they cannot be works of art.

The senator's reasoning contains which one of the following errors?

(A) It seeks to persuade by emotional rather than intellectual means.
(B) It contains an implicit contradiction.
(C) It relies on an assertion of the senator's authority.
(D) It assumes what it seeks to establish.
(E) It attempts to justify a position by appeal to an irrelevant consideration.

9. Until he was dismissed amid great controversy, Hastings was considered one of the greatest intelligence agents of all time. It is clear that if his dismissal was justified, then Hastings was either incompetent or else disloyal. Soon after the dismissal, however, it was shown that he had never been incompetent. Thus, one is forced to conclude that Hastings must have been disloyal.

Which one of the following states an assumption upon which the argument depends?

(A) Hastings's dismissal was justified.
(B) Hastings was a high-ranking intelligence officer.
(C) The dismissal of anyone who was disloyal would be justified.
(D) Anyone whose dismissal was justified was disloyal.
(E) If someone was disloyal or incompetent, then his dismissal was justified.

10. Anyone who fails to answer a patient's questions cannot be a competent physician. That is why I feel confident about my physician's competence: she carefully answers every one of my questions, no matter how trivial.

Which one of the following most closely parallels the flawed reasoning in the argument above?

(A) Anyone who grows up in a large family is accustomed to making compromises. Meredith is accustomed to making compromises, so she might have grown up in a large family.
(B) Anyone who is not in favor of this proposal is ill informed on the issue. Jeanne opposes the proposal, so she is ill informed on the issue.
(C) No one who likes music misses a performance of the symphony. Paul likes music, yet last week he missed a performance of the symphony.
(D) Anyone who works two or more jobs is unable to find a balance between professional and personal life. Maggie has only one job, so she can find a balance between her professional and personal life.
(E) No one who is hot-tempered and strong-willed will succeed in this business. Jeremy is strong-willed, so he will not succeed in this business.

GO ON TO THE NEXT PAGE.

11. The annual *Journal for Publication*, which often solicits articles, publishes only those articles that are both submitted before March 6 and written by certified psychoanalysts. Stevens, who publishes frequently in psychoanalytic literature, submitted an article to the *Journal* before March 6. This article was accepted for publication in the *Journal*.

Which one of the following conclusions follows logically from the statements above?

(A) Stevens is a psychoanalyst.
(B) The *Journal* frequently accepts Stevens' articles.
(C) Stevens is an authority on a large number of topics in psychoanalysis.
(D) The *Journal* asked Stevens to write an article.
(E) Stevens' recently accepted article will be interesting to *Journal* readers.

Questions 12–13

Arguing that there was no trade between Europe and East Asia in the early Middle Ages because there are no written records of such trade is like arguing that the yeti, an apelike creature supposedly existing in the Himalayas, does not exist because there have been no scientifically confirmed sightings. A verifiable sighting of the yeti would prove that the creature does exist, but the absence of sightings cannot prove that it does not.

12. Which one of the following best expresses the point of the argument?

(A) Evidence for the existence of trade between Europe and East Asia in the early Middle Ages is, like evidence for the existence of the yeti, not scientifically confirmed.
(B) In order to prove that in the early Middle Ages there was trade between Europe and East Asia it is necessary to find both Asian and European evidence that such trade existed.
(C) That trade between Europe and East Asia did not exist in the early Middle Ages cannot be established simply by the absence of a certain sort of evidence that this trade existed.
(D) The view that there was trade between Europe and East Asia in the early Middle Ages can only be disproved by showing that no references to this trade exist in surviving records.
(E) There is no more evidence that trade between Europe and East Asia existed in the early Middle Ages than there is that the yeti exists.

13. Which one of the following considerations, if true, best counters the argument?

(A) Most of the evidence for the existence of trade between Europe and East Asia in the early Middle Ages is archaeological and therefore does not rely on written records.
(B) Although written records of trade in East Asia in the early Middle Ages survived, there are almost no European documents from that period that mention trade at all.
(C) Any trade between Europe and East Asia in the early Middle Ages would necessarily have been of very low volume and would have involved high-priced items, such as precious metals and silk.
(D) There have been no confirmed sightings of the yeti, but there is indirect evidence, such as footprints, which if it is accepted as authentic would establish the yeti's existence.
(E) There are surviving European and East Asian written records from the early Middle Ages that do not mention trade between the two regions but would have been very likely to do so if this trade had existed.

GO ON TO THE NEXT PAGE.

14. When the economy is in a recession, overall demand for goods and services is low. If overall demand for goods and services is low, bank interest rates are also low. Therefore, if bank interest rates are not low, the economy is not in a recession.

The reasoning in which one of the following most closely parallels the reasoning in the argument above?

(A) If the restaurant is full, the parking lot will be full, and if the parking lot is full, the restaurant is full, so if the parking lot is not full, the restaurant is not full.

(B) If the fish is ready, it is cooked all the way through, and if it is cooked through it will be white, so if the fish is not white, it is not ready.

(C) If pterodactyls flew by flapping their wings, they must have been warm-blooded, so if they were cold-blooded, they must have flown only by gliding, if they flew at all.

(D) If you want to put in pleats, you will have to double the amount of material for the skirt, and that means you will have none left for the top, so if you put in pleats you will not be able to make the top.

(E) If economic forecasters are right, there will be inflation, and if there is inflation, the governing party will lose the election, so if it does lose the election, the economic forecasters were right.

15. Twenty years ago the Republic of Rosinia produced nearly 100 million tons of potatoes, but last year the harvest barely reached 60 million tons. Agricultural researchers, who have failed to develop new higher-yielding strains of potatoes, are to blame for this decrease, since they have been concerned only with their own research and not with the needs of Rosinia.

Which one of the following is an assumption on which the argument depends?

(A) Any current attempts by agricultural researchers to develop higher-yielding potato strains are futile.

(B) Strains of potatoes most commonly grown in Rosinia could not have produced the yields last year that they once did.

(C) Agricultural researchers often find concrete solutions to practical problems when investigating seemingly unrelated questions.

(D) Wide fluctuations in the size of the potato crop over a twenty-year period are not unusual.

(E) Agricultural research in Rosinia is funded by government grants.

16. An ancient Pavonian text describes how an army of one million enemies of Pavonia stopped to drink at a certain lake and drank the lake dry. Recently, archaeologists discovered that water-based life was suddenly absent just after the event was alleged by the text to have occurred. On the basis of reading the text and an account of the archaeological evidence, some students concluded that the events described really took place.

Which one of the following is a questionable technique used by the students to reach their conclusion?

(A) making a generalization about historical events on the basis of a single instance of that type of event

(B) ignoring available, potentially useful counterevidence

(C) rejecting a hypothesis because it is seemingly self-contradictory

(D) considering people and locations whose existence cannot be substantiated by modern historians

(E) taking evidence that a text has correctly described an effect to show that the text has correctly described the cause

GO ON TO THE NEXT PAGE.

24. Rumored declines in automobile-industry revenues are exaggerated. It is true that automobile manufacturers' share of the industry's revenues fell from 65 percent two years ago to 50 percent today, but over the same period suppliers of automobile parts had their share increase from 15 percent to 20 percent and service companies (for example, distributors, dealers, and repairers) had their share increase from 20 percent to 30 percent.

Which one of the following best indicates why the statistics given above provide by themselves no evidence for the conclusion they are intended to support?

(A) The possibility is left open that the statistics for manufacturers' share of revenues come from a different source than the other statistics.

(B) No matter what changes the automobile industry's overall revenues undergo, the total of all shares of these revenues must be 100 percent.

(C) No explanation is given for why the revenue shares of different sectors of the industry changed.

(D) Manufacturers and parts companies depend for their revenue on dealers' success in selling cars.

(E) Revenues are an important factor but are not the only factor in determining profits.

Questions 25–26

Proposals for extending the United States school year to bring it more in line with its European and Japanese counterparts are often met with the objection that curtailing the schools' three-month summer vacation would violate an established United States tradition dating from the nineteenth century. However, this objection misses its mark. True, in the nineteenth century the majority of schools closed for three months every summer, but only because they were in rural areas where successful harvests depended on children's labor. If any policy could be justified by those appeals to tradition, it would be the policy of determining the length of the school year according to the needs of the economy.

25. Which one of the following principles, if accepted, would provide the strongest justification for the conclusion?

(A) That a given social policy has traditionally been in force justifies maintaining that policy only if doing so does not conflict with more pressing social needs.

(B) Appeals to its own traditions cannot excuse a country from the obligation to bring its practices in line with the legitimate expectations of the rest of the world.

(C) Because appeals to tradition often serve to mask the real interests at issue, such appeals should be disregarded.

(D) Traditional principles should be discarded when they no longer serve the needs of the economy.

(E) The actual tradition embodied in a given practice can be accurately identified only by reference to the reasons that originally prompted that practice.

26. The argument counters the objection by

(A) providing evidence to show that the objection relies on a misunderstanding about the amount of time each year United States schools traditionally have been closed

(B) calling into question the relevance of information about historical practices to current disputes about proposed social change

(C) arguing for an alternative understanding of the nature of the United States tradition regarding the length of the school year

(D) showing that those who oppose extending the school year have no genuine concern for tradition

(E) demonstrating that tradition justifies bringing the United States school year in line with that of the rest of the industrialized world

S T O P

IF YOU FINISH BEFORE TIME IS CALLED, YOU MAY CHECK YOUR WORK ON THIS SECTION ONLY.
DO NOT WORK ON ANY OTHER SECTION IN THE TEST.

SECTION IV

Time—35 minutes

24 Questions

Directions: Each group of questions in this section is based on a set of conditions. In answering some of the questions, it may be useful to draw a rough diagram. Choose the response that most accurately and completely answers each question and blacken the corresponding space on your answer sheet.

Questions 1–6

Petworld has exactly fourteen animals (three gerbils, three hamsters, three lizards, five snakes) that are kept in four separate cages (W, X, Y, Z) according to the following conditions:

Each cage contains exactly two, four, or six animals.
Any cage containing a gerbil also contains at least one hamster; any cage containing a hamster also contains at least one gerbil.
Any cage containing a lizard also contains at least one snake; any cage containing a snake also contains at least one lizard.
Neither cage Y nor cage Z contains a gerbil.
Neither cage W nor cage X contains a lizard.

1. Which one of the following could be a complete and accurate list of the animals kept in cages W and Y ?

    (A) W: one gerbil and one hamster
         Y: two lizards and two snakes
    (B) W: one gerbil and two hamsters
         Y: one lizard and three snakes
    (C) W: two gerbils and two hamsters
         Y: one lizard and four snakes
    (D) W: two gerbils and two hamsters
         Y: three lizards and one snake
    (E) W: two gerbils and two lizards
         Y: two hamsters and two snakes

2. If there are exactly two hamsters in cage W and the number of gerbils in cage X is equal to the number of snakes in cage Y, then the number of snakes in cage Z must be exactly

    (A) one
    (B) two
    (C) three
    (D) four
    (E) five

3. If cage Z contains exactly twice as many lizards as cage Y, which one of the following can be true?

    (A) Cage Y contains exactly two lizards.
    (B) Cage Y contains exactly two snakes.
    (C) Cage Y contains exactly four animals.
    (D) Cage Z contains exactly three snakes.
    (E) Cage Z contains exactly two animals.

4. If the number of animals in cage W is equal to the number of animals in cage Z, then which one of the following can be true?

    (A) Cage W contains exactly six animals.
    (B) Cage X contains exactly six animals.
    (C) Cage Y contains exactly one snake.
    (D) Cage Y contains exactly three snakes.
    (E) Cage Z contains exactly four snakes.

5. If cage Y contains six animals, which one of the following must be true?

    (A) Cage W contains two gerbils.
    (B) Cage X contains four animals.
    (C) Cage Z contains two snakes.
    (D) The number of snakes in cage Y is equal to the number of lizards in cage Y.
    (E) The number of snakes in cage Z is equal to the number of lizards in cage Z.

6. At most, how many snakes can occupy cage Y at any one time?

    (A) one
    (B) two
    (C) three
    (D) four
    (E) five

GO ON TO THE NEXT PAGE.

Questions 7–12

A soft drink manufacturer surveyed consumer preferences for exactly seven proposed names for its new soda: Jazz, Kola, Luck, Mist, Nipi, Oboy, and Ping. The manufacturer ranked the seven names according to the number of votes they received. The name that received the most votes was ranked first. Every name received a different number of votes. Some of the survey results are as follows:

Jazz received more votes than Oboy.
Oboy received more votes than Kola.
Kola received more votes than Mist.
Nipi did not receive the fewest votes.
Ping received fewer votes than Luck but more votes than Nipi and more votes than Oboy.

7. Which one of the following could be an accurate list of the seven names in rank order from first through seventh?

(A) Jazz, Luck, Ping, Nipi, Kola, Oboy, Mist
(B) Jazz, Luck, Ping, Oboy, Kola, Mist, Nipi
(C) Luck, Ping, Jazz, Nipi, Oboy, Kola, Mist
(D) Luck, Ping, Nipi, Oboy, Jazz, Kola, Mist
(E) Ping, Luck, Jazz, Oboy, Nipi, Kola, Mist

8. Which one of the following statements must be true?

(A) Jazz received more votes than Nipi.
(B) Kola received more votes than Nipi.
(C) Luck received more votes than Jazz.
(D) Nipi received more votes than Oboy.
(E) Ping received more votes than Kola.

9. If the ranks of Ping, Oboy, and Kola were consecutive, then which one of the following statements would have to be false?

(A) Jazz received more votes than Luck.
(B) Jazz received more votes than Ping.
(C) Nipi received more votes than Oboy.
(D) Nipi received more votes than Mist.
(E) Oboy received more votes than Nipi.

10. What is the total number of the soft drink names whose exact ranks can be deduced from the partial survey results?

(A) one
(B) two
(C) three
(D) four
(E) five

11. What is the maximum possible number of the soft drink names any one of which could be among the three most popular?

(A) three
(B) four
(C) five
(D) six
(E) seven

12. If Ping received more votes than Jazz, then what is the maximum possible number of names whose ranks can be determined?

(A) two
(B) three
(C) four
(D) five
(E) six

GO ON TO THE NEXT PAGE.

Questions 13–19

Eight benches—J, K, L, T, U, X, Y, and Z—are arranged along the perimeter of a park as shown below:

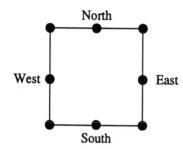

The following is true:
  J, K, and L are green; T and U are red; X, Y, and Z are pink.
  The green benches stand next to one another along the park's perimeter.
  The pink benches stand next to one another along the park's perimeter.
  No green bench stands next to a pink bench.
  The bench on the southeast corner is T.
  J stands at the center of the park's north side.
  If T stands next to X, then T does not also stand next to L.

13. Which one of the following benches could be on the northeast corner of the park?

    (A) Z
    (B) Y
    (C) X
    (D) T
    (E) L

14. Each of the following statements must be true EXCEPT:

    (A) The bench on the northwest corner is pink.
    (B) The bench on the northeast corner is green.
    (C) The bench on the southwest corner is pink.
    (D) The middle bench on the east side of the park is green.
    (E) The middle bench on the west side of the park is pink.

15. Which one of the following benches must be next to J?

    (A) K
    (B) L
    (C) T
    (D) U
    (E) X

16. For which one of the following benches are there two and no more than two locations either one of which could be the location the bench occupies?

    (A) K
    (B) T
    (C) X
    (D) Y
    (E) Z

17. If Z is directly north of Y, which one of the following statements must be true?

    (A) J is directly west of K.
    (B) K is directly east of U.
    (C) U is directly north of X.
    (D) X is directly south of J.
    (E) Z is directly south of J.

18. If Y is in the middle of the west side of the park, then the two benches in which one of the following pairs CANNOT be two of the corner benches?

    (A) K and X
    (B) K and Z
    (C) L and U
    (D) L and X
    (E) L and Z

19. If Y is farther south than L and farther north than T, then the benches in each of the following pairs must be next to each other EXCEPT

    (A) J and L
    (B) K and T
    (C) T and X
    (D) U and Y
    (E) X and Z

GO ON TO THE NEXT PAGE.

Questions 20–24

A lake contains exactly five islands—J, K, L, M, O—which are unconnected by bridges. Contractors will build a network of bridges that satisfies the following specifications:

Each bridge directly connects exactly two islands with each other, and no two bridges intersect.

No more than one bridge directly connects any two islands.

No island has more than three bridges that directly connect it with other islands.

J, K, and L are each directly connected by bridge with one or both of M and O.

J is directly connected by bridge with exactly two islands.

K is directly connected by bridge with exactly one island.

A bridge directly connects J with O, and a bridge directly connects M with O.

20. Which one of the following is a complete and accurate list of the islands any one of which could be directly connected by bridge with L ?

   (A) J, K
   (B) J, M
   (C) J, O
   (D) J, M, O
   (E) J, K, M, O

21. Which one of the following could be true about the completed network of bridges?

   (A) J is directly connected by bridge both with L and with M.
   (B) K is directly connected by bridge both with M and with O.
   (C) L is directly connected by bridge both with J and with M.
   (D) M is directly connected by bridge with J, with K, and with L.
   (E) O is directly connected by bridge with K, with L, and with M.

22. If a bridge directly connects K with O, then which one of the following could be true?

   (A) No bridge directly connects L with M.
   (B) A bridge directly connects J with L.
   (C) A bridge directly connects L with O.
   (D) There are exactly three bridges directly connecting L with other islands.
   (E) There are exactly two bridges directly connecting O with other islands.

23. If a bridge directly connects L with M and a bridge directly connects L with O, then which one of the following must be true?

   (A) A bridge directly connects J with M.
   (B) A bridge directly connects K with M.
   (C) A bridge directly connects K with O.
   (D) There are exactly two bridges directly connecting L with other islands.
   (E) There are exactly two bridges directly connecting M with other islands.

24. If no island that is directly connected by bridge with M is also directly connected by bridge with O, then there must be a bridge directly connecting

   (A) J with L
   (B) J with M
   (C) K with O
   (D) L with M
   (E) L with O

S T O P

IF YOU FINISH BEFORE TIME IS CALLED, YOU MAY CHECK YOUR WORK ON THIS SECTION ONLY.
DO NOT WORK ON ANY OTHER SECTION IN THE TEST.

SIGNATURE ——————————————————————————

LSAT WRITING SAMPLE TOPIC

Green Earth, an organization devoted to preserving the environment, has decided to expand its activities into the field of publishing. Write an argument in favor of selecting one or the other of the following manuscripts as the organization's inaugural publication. Consider the following when making your decision:

- Green Earth wishes to develop a reputation as a publishing house for scholarly and influential works on the environment.
- Green Earth is financially dependent on the voluntary contributions of its supporters and hopes to raise significant funds through proceeds from the book.

John Dailey, a journalist who has spent most of his career travelling the world in order to gain first-hand knowledge of environmental issues, has submitted a collection of essays discussing both his experiences and a variety of environmental problems. Dailey's work has always been extremely popular, and his book would likely prove one of the few accessible texts addressing the difficult scientific issues underlying many of today's environmental questions. Despite his extensive experience and careful research, several scholars have recently expressed concern about the scientific accuracy of some of Dailey's reports. Dailey, currently researching a new article on herbal medicines obtained from an endangered plant species in the Amazon rain forest, has not yet had time to prepare a response.

Ginny Fredericks, a professor and author of several well-known scientific studies of environmental issues, has submitted a manuscript proposing a sweeping plan of action for preserving the environment. Dr. Fredericks' reputation as a scientist guarantees that the book, the crowning achievement of her long and distinguished career, will receive a significant amount of media attention. However, those accustomed to her impartial approach to environmental questions may be taken aback and perhaps outraged by her impassioned argument for a very radical program of action. Dr. Fredericks has volunteered to donate a percentage of the proceeds from a lecture tour she plans in conjunction with her book to the book's publisher, but William Stone, a noted philanthropist and long-time supporter of Green Earth, has expressed concern over the organization's support of such a potentially controversial figure.

Directions:

1. Use the Answer Key on the next page to check your answers.

2. Use the Scoring Worksheet below to compute your raw score.

3. Use the Score Conversion Chart to convert your raw score into the 120-180 scale.

Scoring Worksheet

1. Enter the number of questions you answered correctly in each section.

	Number Correct
SECTION I	_____
SECTION II	_____
SECTION III	_____
SECTION IV	_____

2. Enter the sum here: _____

   This is your Raw Score.

Conversion Chart
Form K-2LSS14

For Converting Raw Score to the 120-180 LSAT Scaled Score

Reported Score	Raw Score Lowest	Raw Score Highest
180	100	102
179	—*	—*
178	99	99
177	98	98
176	97	97
175	96	96
174	95	95
173	94	94
172	93	93
171	92	92
170	91	91
169	90	90
168	88	89
167	87	87
166	85	86
165	84	84
164	82	83
163	80	81
162	79	79
161	77	78
160	75	76
159	73	74
158	72	72
157	70	71
156	68	69
155	66	67
154	64	65
153	62	63
152	61	61
151	59	60
150	57	58
149	55	56
148	53	54
147	51	52
146	50	50
145	48	49
144	46	47
143	44	45
142	42	43
141	41	41
140	39	40
139	37	38
138	36	36
137	34	35
136	33	33
135	31	32
134	29	30
133	28	28
132	27	27
131	25	26
130	24	24
129	23	23
128	22	22
127	20	21
126	19	19
125	18	18
124	17	17
123	16	16
122	—*	—*
121	15	15
120	0	14

*There is no raw score that will produce this scaled score for this form.

SECTION I

1.	E	8.	D	15.	D	22.	A
2.	C	9.	A	16.	B	23.	C
3.	A	10.	A	17.	B	24.	E
4.	E	11.	D	18.	D	25.	E
5.	B	12.	D	19.	D	26.	A
6.	D	13.	D	20.	C	27.	E
7.	E	14.	A	21.	C		

SECTION II

1.	C	8.	A	15.	C	22.	D
2.	A	9.	C	16.	E	23.	E
3.	D	10.	E	17.	B	24.	C
4.	E	11.	B	18.	E	25.	C
5.	B	12.	E	19.	E		
6.	C	13.	E	20.	C		
7.	E	14.	D	21.	D		

SECTION III

1.	A	8.	D	15.	B	22.	A
2.	B	9.	A	16.	E	23.	D
3.	D	10.	D	17.	A	24.	B
4.	B	11.	A	18.	A	25.	E
5.	D	12.	C	19.	D	26.	C
6.	E	13.	E	20.	C		
7.	A	14.	B	21.	E		

SECTION IV

1.	A	8.	E	15.	D	22.	B
2.	D	9.	C	16.	A	23.	B
3.	C	10.	A	17.	D	24.	A
4.	D	11.	B	18.	B		
5.	E	12.	B	19.	C		
6.	D	13.	E	20.	D		
7.	C	14.	A	21.	C		

The Official

LSAT

PrepTest™ VII

The sample test that follows consists of four sections corresponding to the four scored sections of the February 1993 LSAT.

February 1993
Form 3LSS18

INSTRUCTIONS FOR COMPLETING THE BIOGRAPHICAL AREA ARE ON THE BACK COVER OF YOUR TEST BOOKLET.
USE ONLY A NO. 2 OR HB PENCIL TO COMPLETE THIS ANSWER SHEET. DO NOT USE INK.

1 LAST NAME / FIRST NAME / MI

(A–Z bubble grid for last name, first name, and middle initial)

2 DATE OF BIRTH

MONTH	DAY	YEAR
Jan, Feb, Mar, Apr, May, June, July, Aug, Sept, Oct, Nov, Dec	(0–9 bubbles)	(0–9 bubbles)

3 SOCIAL SECURITY NO.

(0–9 bubble grid)

Right Mark: ●
Wrong Marks: ⊘ ⊗ ⊙

4 ETHNIC DESCRIPTION

- American Indian/Alaskan Native
- Asian/Pacific Islander
- Black/African Amer.
- Canadian Aboriginal
- Caucasian/White
- Chicano/Mex. Amer.
- Hispanic
- Puerto Rican
- Other

5 GENDER
- Male
- Female

6 DOMINANT LANGUAGE
- English
- Other

7 ENGLISH FLUENCY
- Yes
- No

8 CENTER NUMBER (0–9 bubbles)

9 TEST FORM CODE (0–9 bubbles)

10 TEST BOOK SERIAL NO.

11 TEST FORM

12 TEST DATE MONTH / DAY / YEAR

13 PLEASE PRINT ALL INFORMATION

LAST NAME ___ FIRST ___
MAILING ADDRESS ___
SOCIAL SECURITY/SOCIAL INSURANCE NO. ___

LAW SCHOOL ADMISSION TEST

MARK ONE AND ONLY ONE ANSWER TO EACH QUESTION. BE SURE TO FILL IN COMPLETELY THE SPACE FOR YOUR INTENDED ANSWER CHOICE. IF YOU ERASE, DO SO COMPLETELY. MAKE NO STRAY MARKS.

SECTION 1 / SECTION 2 / SECTION 3 / SECTION 4 / SECTION 5

Questions 1–30, each with answer choices (A) (B) (C) (D) (E)

NOTE: If you have a new address, you must write Law Services at Box 2000-C, Newtown, PA 18940 or call (215) 968-1001. We cannot guarantee that all address changes will be processed before scores are mailed, so be sure to notify your post office of your forwarding address.

FOR LAW SERVICES USE ONLY
LR
LW
LCS

Copyright © 1994 BY LAW SCHOOL ADMISSION SERVICES, INC. ALL RIGHTS RESERVED. PRINTED IN U.S.A.

General Directions for the LSAT Answer Sheet

The actual testing time for this portion of the test will be 2 hours 55 minutes. There are five sections, each with a time limit of 35 minutes. The supervisor will tell you when to begin and end each section. If you finish a section before time is called, you may check your work on that section <u>only</u>; do not turn to any other section of the test book and do not work on any other section either in the test book or on the answer sheet.

There are several different types of questions on the test, and each question type has its own directions. <u>Be sure you understand the directions for each question type before attempting to answer any questions in that section.</u>

Not everyone will finish all the questions in the time allowed. Do not hurry, but work steadily and as quickly as you can without sacrificing accuracy. You are advised to use your time effectively. If a question seems too difficult, go on to the next one and return to the difficult question after completing the section. MARK THE BEST ANSWER YOU CAN FOR EVERY QUESTION. NO DEDUCTIONS WILL BE MADE FOR WRONG ANSWERS. YOUR SCORE WILL BE BASED ONLY ON THE NUMBER OF QUESTIONS YOU ANSWER CORRECTLY.

ALL YOUR ANSWERS MUST BE MARKED ON THE ANSWER SHEET. Answer spaces for each question are lettered to correspond with the letters of the potential answers to each question in the test book. After you have decided which of the answers is correct, blacken the corresponding space on the answer sheet. BE SURE THAT EACH MARK IS BLACK AND COMPLETELY FILLS THE ANSWER SPACE. Give only one answer to each question. If you change an answer, be sure that all previous marks are <u>erased completely</u>. Since the answer sheet is machine scored, incomplete erasures may be interpreted as intended answers. ANSWERS RECORDED IN THE TEST BOOK WILL NOT BE SCORED.

There may be more questions noted on this answer sheet than there are questions in a section. Do not be concerned but be certain that the section and number of the question you are answering matches the answer sheet section and question number. Additional answer spaces in any answer sheet section should be left blank. Begin your next section in the number one answer space for that section.

Score Cancellation

Complete this section only if you are absolutely certain you want to cancel your score. A CANCELLATION REQUEST CANNOT BE RESCINDED. IF YOU ARE AT ALL UNCERTAIN, YOU SHOULD NOT COMPLETE THIS SECTION; INSTEAD, YOU SHOULD USE THE TIME ALLOWED AFTER THE TEST (UP TO 5 DAYS) TO FULLY CONSIDER YOUR DECISION.

To cancel your score from this administration, you must:

A. fill in the ovals here........ ◯ ◯

B. read the following statement. Then sign your name and enter the date.

I certify that I wish to cancel my test score from this administration. I understand that my request is irreversible and that my score will not be sent to me or to the law schools to which I apply.

_____

Sign your name in full

_____

Date

HOW DID YOU PREPARE FOR THE LSAT?
(Select all that apply.)

Responses to this item are voluntary and will be used for statistical research purposes only.

◯ By studying the sample questions in the *LSAT/LSDAS Registration and Information Book*.
◯ By taking the free sample LSAT.
◯ By working through *The Official LSAT PrepTest(s), PrepBook, Workbooks, or PrepKit*.
◯ By using a book on how to prepare for the LSAT **not** published by Law Services.
◯ By attending a commercial test preparation or coaching course.
◯ By attending a test preparation or coaching course offered through an undergraduate institution.
◯ Self study.
◯ Other preparation.
◯ No preparation.

CERTIFYING STATEMENT

Please write (DO NOT PRINT) the following statement. Sign and date.

I certify that I am the examinee whose name appears on this answer sheet and that I am here to take the LSAT for the sole purpose of being considered for admission to law school. I further certify that I will neither assist nor receive assistance from any other candidate, and I agree not to copy or retain examination questions or to transmit them in any form to any other person.

_____

_____

_____

_____

_____

_____

_____

_____

_____

SIGNATURE: _____   TODAY'S DATE: _____ / _____ / _____

MONTH   DAY   YEAR

SECTION I

Time—35 minutes

25 Questions

Directions: The questions in this section are based on the reasoning contained in brief statements or passages. For some questions, more than one of the choices could conceivably answer the question. However, you are to choose the best answer; that is, the response that most accurately and completely answers the question. You should not make assumptions that are by commonsense standards implausible, superfluous, or incompatible with the passage. After you have chosen the best answer, blacken the corresponding space on your answer sheet.

1. Before the printing press, books could be purchased only in expensive manuscript copies. The printing press produced books that were significantly less expensive than the manuscript editions. The public's demand for printed books in the first years after the invention of the printing press was many times greater than demand had been for manuscript copies. This increase demonstrates that there was a dramatic jump in the number of people who learned how to read in the years after publishers first started producing books on the printing press.

   Which one of the following statements, if true, casts doubt on the argument?

   (A) During the first years after the invention of the printing press, letter writing by people who wrote without the assistance of scribes or clerks exhibited a dramatic increase.
   (B) Books produced on the printing press are often found with written comments in the margins in the handwriting of the people who owned the books.
   (C) In the first years after the printing press was invented, printed books were purchased primarily by people who had always bought and read expensive manuscripts but could afford a greater number of printed books for the same money.
   (D) Books that were printed on the printing press in the first years after its invention often circulated among friends in informal reading clubs or libraries.
   (E) The first printed books published after the invention of the printing press would have been useless to illiterate people, since the books had virtually no illustrations.

2. Bevex, an artificial sweetener used only in soft drinks, is carcinogenic for mice, but only when it is consumed in very large quantities. To ingest an amount of Bevex equivalent to the amount fed to the mice in the relevant studies, a person would have to drink 25 cans of Bevex-sweetened soft drinks per day. For that reason, Bevex is in fact safe for people.

   In order for the conclusion that Bevex is safe for people to be properly drawn, which one of the following must be true?

   (A) Cancer from carcinogenic substances develops more slowly in mice than it does in people.
   (B) If all food additives that are currently used in foods were tested, some would be found to be carcinogenic for mice.
   (C) People drink fewer than 25 cans of Bevex-sweetened soda per day.
   (D) People can obtain important health benefits by controlling their weight through the use of artificially sweetened soft drinks.
   (E) Some of the studies done on Bevex were not relevant to the question of whether or not Bevex is carcinogenic for people.

3. Harry: Airlines have made it possible for anyone to travel around the world in much less time than was formerly possible.
   Judith: That is not true. Many flights are too expensive for all but the rich.

   Judith's response shows that she interprets Harry's statement to imply that

   (A) the majority of people are rich
   (B) everyone has an equal right to experience world travel
   (C) world travel is only possible via routes serviced by airlines
   (D) most forms of world travel are not affordable for most people
   (E) anyone can afford to travel long distances by air

GO ON TO THE NEXT PAGE.

4. Nutritionists have recommended that people eat more fiber. Advertisements for a new fiber-supplement pill state only that it contains "44 percent fiber."

The advertising claim is misleading in its selection of information on which to focus if which one of the following is true?

(A) There are other products on the market that are advertised as providing fiber as a dietary supplement.
(B) Nutritionists base their recommendation on medical findings that dietary fiber protects against some kinds of cancer.
(C) It is possible to become addicted to some kinds of advertised pills, such as sleeping pills and painkillers.
(D) The label of the advertised product recommends taking 3 pills every day.
(E) The recommended daily intake of fiber is 20 to 30 grams, and the pill contains one-third gram.

5. Many environmentalists have urged environmental awareness on consumers, saying that if we accept moral responsibility for our effects on the environment, then products that directly or indirectly harm the environment ought to be avoided. Unfortunately it is usually impossible for consumers to assess the environmental impact of a product, and thus impossible for them to consciously restrict their purchases to environmentally benign products. Because of this impossibility there can be no moral duty to choose products in the way these environmentalists urge, since _____.

Which one of the following principles provides the most appropriate completion for the argument?

(A) a moral duty to perform an action is never based solely on the effects the action will have on other people
(B) a person cannot possibly have a moral duty to do what he or she is unable to do
(C) moral considerations should not be the sole determinants of what products are made available to consumers
(D) the morally right action is always the one whose effects produce the least total harm
(E) where a moral duty exists, it supersedes any legal duty and any other kind of duty

6. Advertisement: Anyone who exercises knows from firsthand experience that exercise leads to better performance of such physical organs as the heart and the lungs, as well as to improvement in muscle tone. And since your brain is a physical organ, your actions can improve its performance, too. Act now. Subscribe to *Stimulus*: read the magazine that exercises your brain.

The advertisement employs which one of the following argumentative strategies?

(A) It cites experimental evidence that subscribing to the product being advertised has desirable consequences.
(B) It ridicules people who do not subscribe to *Stimulus* by suggesting that they do not believe that exercise will improve brain capacity.
(C) It explains the process by which the product being advertised brings about the result claimed for its use.
(D) It supports its recommendation by a careful analysis of the concept of exercise.
(E) It implies that brains and muscle are similar in one respect because they are similar in another respect.

GO ON TO THE NEXT PAGE.

Questions 7-8

Coherent solutions for the problem of reducing health-care costs cannot be found within the current piecemeal system of paying these costs. The reason is that this system gives health-care providers and insurers every incentive to shift, wherever possible, the costs of treating illness onto each other or any other party, including the patient. That clearly is the lesson of the various reforms of the 1980s: push in on one part of this pliable spending balloon and an equally expensive bulge pops up elsewhere. For example, when the government health-care insurance program for the poor cut costs by disallowing payments for some visits to physicians, patients with advanced illness later presented themselves at hospital emergency rooms in increased numbers.

7. The argument proceeds by

    (A) showing that shifting costs onto the patient contradicts the premise of health-care reimbursement
    (B) attributing without justification fraudulent intent to people
    (C) employing an analogy to characterize interrelationships
    (D) denying the possibility of a solution by disparaging each possible alternative system
    (E) demonstrating that cooperation is feasible by citing an instance

8. The argument provides the most support for which one of the following?

    (A) Under the conditions in which the current system operates, the overall volume of health-care costs could be shrunk, if at all, only by a comprehensive approach.
    (B) Relative to the resources available for health-care funding, the income of the higher-paid health-care professionals is too high.
    (C) Health-care costs are expanding to meet additional funds that have been made available for them.
    (D) Advances in medical technology have raised the expected standards of medical care but have proved expensive.
    (E) Since unfilled hospital beds contribute to overhead charges on each patient's bill, it would be unwise to hold unused hospital capacity in reserve for large-scale emergencies.

9. The commercial news media emphasize exceptional events such as airplane crashes at the expense of those such as automobile accidents, which occur far more frequently and represent a far greater risk to the public. Yet the public tends to interpret the degree of emphasis the news media give to these occurrences as indicating the degree of risk they represent.

    If the statements above are true, which one of the following conclusions is most strongly supported by them?

    (A) Print media, such as newspapers and magazines, are a better source of information than are broadcast media.
    (B) The emphasis given in the commercial news media to major catastrophes is dictated by the public's taste for the extraordinary.
    (C) Events over which people feel they have no control are generally perceived as more dangerous than those which people feel they can avert or avoid.
    (D) Where commercial news media constitute the dominant source of information, public perception of risk does not reflect actual risk.
    (E) A massive outbreak of cholera will be covered more extensively by the news media than will the occurrence of a rarer but less serious disease.

10. A large group of hyperactive children whose regular diets included food containing large amounts of additives was observed by researchers trained to assess the presence or absence of behavior problems. The children were then placed on a low-additive diet for several weeks, after which they were observed again. Originally nearly 60 percent of the children exhibited behavior problems; after the change in diet, only 30 percent did so. On the basis of these data, it can be concluded that food additives can contribute to behavior problems in hyperactive children.

    The evidence cited fails to establish the conclusion because

    (A) there is no evidence that the reduction in behavior problems was proportionate to the reduction in food-additive intake
    (B) there is no way to know what changes would have occurred without the change of diet, since only children who changed to a low-additive diet were studied
    (C) exactly how many children exhibited behavior problems after the change in diet cannot be determined, since the size of the group studied is not precisely given
    (D) there is no evidence that the behavior of some of the children was unaffected by additives
    (E) the evidence is consistent with the claim that some children exhibit more frequent behavior problems after being on the low-additive diet than they had exhibited when first observed

GO ON TO THE NEXT PAGE.

11. In 1990 major engine repairs were performed on 10 percent of the cars that had been built by the National Motor Company in the 1970s and that were still registered. However, the corresponding figure for the cars that the National Motor Company had manufactured in the 1960s was only five percent.

Which one of the following, if true, most helps to explain the discrepancy?

(A) Government motor vehicle regulations generally require all cars, whether old or new, to be inspected for emission levels prior to registration.

(B) Owners of new cars tend to drive their cars more carefully than do owners of old cars.

(C) The older a car is, the more likely it is to be discarded for scrap rather than repaired when major engine work is needed to keep the car in operation.

(D) The cars that the National Motor Company built in the 1970s incorporated simplified engine designs that made the engines less complicated than those of earlier models.

(E) Many of the repairs that were performed on the cars that the National Motor Company built in the 1960s could have been avoided if periodic routine maintenance had been performed.

12. No mathematician today would flatly refuse to accept the results of an enormous computation as an adequate demonstration of the truth of a theorem. In 1976, however, this was not the case. Some mathematicians at that time refused to accept the results of a complex computer demonstration of a very simple mapping theorem. Although some mathematicians still hold a strong belief that a simple theorem ought to have a short, simple proof, in fact, some simple theorems have required enormous proofs.

If all of the statements in the passage are true, which one of the following must also be true?

(A) Today, some mathematicians who believe that a simple theorem ought to have a simple proof would consider accepting the results of an enormous computation as a demonstration of the truth of a theorem.

(B) Some individuals who believe that a simple theorem ought to have a simple proof are not mathematicians.

(C) Today, some individuals who refuse to accept the results of an enormous computation as a demonstration of the truth of a theorem believe that a simple theorem ought to have a simple proof.

(D) Some individuals who do not believe that a simple theorem ought to have a simple proof would not be willing to accept the results of an enormous computation as proof of a complex theorem.

(E) Some nonmathematicians do not believe that a simple theorem ought to have a simple proof.

13. If you climb mountains, you will not live to a ripe old age. But you will be bored unless you climb mountains. Therefore, if you live to a ripe old age, you will have been bored.

Which one of the following most closely parallels the reasoning in the argument above?

(A) If you do not try to swim, you will not learn how to swim. But you will not be safe in boats if you do not learn how to swim. Therefore, you must try to swim.

(B) If you do not play golf, you will not enjoy the weekend. But you will be tired next week unless you relax during the weekend. Therefore, to enjoy the weekend, you will have to relax by playing golf.

(C) If you work for your candidate, you will not improve your guitar playing. But you will neglect your civic duty unless you work for your candidate. Therefore, if you improve your guitar playing, you will have neglected your civic duty.

(D) If you do not train, you will not be a good athlete. But you will become exhausted easily unless you train. Therefore, if you train, you will not have become exhausted easily.

(E) If you spend all of your money, you will not become wealthy. But you will become hungry unless you spend all of your money. Therefore, if you become wealthy, you will not become hungry.

14. Marine biologists had hypothesized that lobsters kept together in lobster traps eat one another in response to hunger. Periodic checking of lobster traps, however, has revealed instances of lobsters sharing traps together for weeks. Eight lobsters even shared one trap together for two months without eating one another. The marine biologists' hypothesis, therefore, is clearly wrong.

The argument against the marine biologists' hypothesis is based on which one of the following assumptions?

(A) Lobsters not caught in lobster traps have been observed eating one another.

(B) Two months is the longest known period during which eight or more lobsters have been trapped together.

(C) It is unusual to find as many as eight lobsters caught together in one single trap.

(D) Members of other marine species sometimes eat their own kind when no other food sources are available.

(E) Any food that the eight lobsters in the trap might have obtained was not enough to ward off hunger.

GO ON TO THE NEXT PAGE.

15. Eight years ago hunting was banned in Greenfield County on the grounds that hunting endangers public safety. Now the deer population in the county is six times what it was before the ban. Deer are invading residential areas, damaging property and causing motor vehicle accidents that result in serious injury to motorists. Since there were never any hunting-related injuries in the county, clearly the ban was not only unnecessary but has created a danger to public safety that would not otherwise exist.

Which one of the following, if true, provides the strongest additional support for the conclusion above?

(A) In surrounding counties, where hunting is permitted, the size of the deer population has not increased in the last eight years.
(B) Motor vehicle accidents involving deer often result in damage to the vehicle, injury to the motorist, or both.
(C) When deer populations increase beyond optimal size, disease and malnutrition become more widespread among the deer herds.
(D) In residential areas in the county, many residents provide food and salt for deer.
(E) Deer can cause extensive damage to ornamental shrubs and trees by chewing on twigs and saplings.

16. Comets do not give off their own light but reflect light from other sources, such as the Sun. Scientists estimate the mass of comets by their brightness: the greater a comet's mass, the more light that comet will reflect. A satellite probe, however, has revealed that the material of which Halley's comet is composed reflects 60 times less light per unit of mass than had been previously thought.

The statements above, if true, give the most support to which one of the following?

(A) Some comets are composed of material that reflects 60 times more light per unit of mass than the material of which Halley's comet is composed.
(B) Previous estimates of the mass of Halley's comet which were based on its brightness were too low.
(C) The total amount of light reflected from Halley's comet is less than scientists had previously thought.
(D) The reflective properties of the material of which comets are composed vary considerably from comet to comet.
(E) Scientists need more information before they can make a good estimate of the mass of Halley's comet.

17. Office manager: I will not order recycled paper for this office. Our letters to clients must make a good impression, so we cannot print them on inferior paper.
Stationery supplier: Recycled paper is not necessarily inferior. In fact, from the beginning, the finest paper has been made of recycled material. It was only in the 1850s that paper began to be made from wood fiber, and then only because there were no longer enough rags to meet the demand for paper.

In which one of the following ways does the stationer's response fail to address the office manager's objection to recycled paper?

(A) It does not recognize that the office manager's prejudice against recycled paper stems from ignorance.
(B) It uses irrelevant facts to justify a claim about the quality of the disputed product.
(C) It assumes that the office manager is concerned about environmental issues.
(D) It presupposes that the office manager understands the basic technology of paper manufacturing.
(E) It ignores the office manager's legitimate concern about quality.

GO ON TO THE NEXT PAGE.

Questions 18–19

When Alicia Green borrowed a neighbor's car without permission, the police merely gave her a warning. However, when Peter Foster did the same thing, he was charged with automobile theft. Peter came to the attention of the police because the car he was driving was hit by a speeding taxi. Alicia was stopped because the car she was driving had defective taillights. It is true that the car Peter took got damaged and the car Alicia took did not, but since it was the taxi that caused the damage this difference was not due to any difference in the blameworthiness of their behavior. Therefore Alicia should also have been charged with automobile theft.

18. The statement that the car Peter took got damaged and the car Alicia took did not plays which one of the following roles in the argument?

   (A) It presents a reason that directly supports the conclusion.
   (B) It justifies the difference in the actual outcome in the two cases.
   (C) It demonstrates awareness of a fact on which a possible objection might be based.
   (D) It illustrates a general principle on which the argument relies.
   (E) It summarizes a position against which the argument is directed.

19. If all of the claims offered in support of the conclusion are accurate, each of the following could be true EXCEPT:

   (A) The interests of justice would have been better served if the police had released Peter Foster with a warning.
   (B) Alicia Green had never before driven a car belonging to someone else without first securing the owner's permission.
   (C) Peter Foster was hit by the taxi while he was running a red light, whereas Alicia Green drove with extra care to avoid drawing the attention of the police to the car she had taken.
   (D) Alicia Green barely missed hitting a pedestrian when she sped through a red light ten minutes before she was stopped by the police for driving a car that had defective taillights.
   (E) Peter Foster had been cited for speeding twice in the preceding month, whereas Alicia Green had never been cited for a traffic violation.

20. According to sources who can be expected to know, Dr. Maria Esposito is going to run in the mayoral election. But if Dr. Esposito runs, Jerome Krasman will certainly not run against her. Therefore Dr. Esposito will be the only candidate in the election.

The flawed reasoning in the argument above most closely parallels that in which one of the following?

   (A) According to its management, Brown's Stores will move next year. Without Brown's being present, no new large store can be attracted to the downtown area. Therefore the downtown area will no longer be viable as a shopping district.
   (B) The press release says that the rock group Rollercoaster is playing a concert on Saturday. It won't be playing on Friday if it plays on Saturday. So Saturday will be the only day this week on which Rollercoaster will perform.
   (C) Joshua says the interviewing panel was impressed by Marilyn. But if they were impressed by Marilyn, they probably thought less of Sven. Joshua is probably right, and so Sven will probably not get the job.
   (D) An informant says that Rustimann was involved in the bank robbery. If Rustimann was involved, Jones was certainly not involved. Since these two are the only people who could have been involved, Rustimann is the only person the police need to arrest.
   (E) The review said that this book is the best one for beginners at programming. If this book is the best, that other one can't be as good. So this one is the book we should buy.

GO ON TO THE NEXT PAGE.

21. The initial causes of serious accidents at nuclear power plants have not so far been flaws in the advanced-technology portion of the plants. Rather, the initial causes have been attributed to human error, as when a worker at the Browns Mills reactor in the United States dropped a candle and started a fire, or to flaws in the plumbing, exemplified in a recent incident in Japan. Such everyday events cannot be thought unlikely to occur over the long run.

Which one of the following is most strongly supported by the statements above?

(A) Now that nuclear power generation has become a part of everyday life, an ever-increasing yearly incidence of serious accidents at the plants can be expected.

(B) If nuclear power plants continue in operation, a serious accident at such a plant is not improbable.

(C) The likelihood of human error at the operating consoles of nuclear power generators cannot be lessened by thoughtful design of dials, switches, and displays.

(D) The design of nuclear power plants attempts to compensate for possible failures of the materials used in their construction.

(E) No serious accident will be caused in the future by some flaw in the advanced-technology portion of a nuclear power plant.

22. There is a widespread belief that people can predict impending earthquakes from unusual animal behavior. Skeptics claim that this belief is based on selective coincidence: people whose dogs behaved oddly just before an earthquake will be especially likely to remember that fact. At any given time, the skeptics say, some of the world's dogs will be behaving oddly.

Clarification of which one of the following issues would be most important to an evaluation of the skeptics' position?

(A) Which is larger, the number of skeptics or the number of people who believe that animal behavior can foreshadow earthquakes?

(B) Are there means other than the observation of animal behavior that nonscientists can use to predict earthquakes?

(C) Are there animals about whose behavior people know too little to be able to distinguish unusual from everyday behavior?

(D) Are the sorts of behavior supposedly predictive of earthquakes as pronounced in dogs as they are in other animals?

(E) Is the animal behavior supposedly predictive of earthquakes specific to impending earthquakes or can it be any kind of unusual behavior?

23. Defendants who can afford expensive private defense lawyers have a lower conviction rate than those who rely on court-appointed public defenders. This explains why criminals who commit lucrative crimes like embezzlement or insider trading are more successful at avoiding conviction than are street criminals.

The explanation offered above would be more persuasive if which one of the following were true?

(A) Many street crimes, such as drug dealing, are extremely lucrative and those committing them can afford expensive private lawyers.

(B) Most prosecutors are not competent to handle cases involving highly technical financial evidence and have more success in prosecuting cases of robbery or simple assault.

(C) The number of criminals convicted of street crimes is far greater than the number of criminals convicted of embezzlement or insider trading.

(D) The percentage of defendants who actually committed the crimes of which they are accused is no greater for publicly defended than for privately defended defendants.

(E) Juries, out of sympathy for the victims of crimes, are much more likely to convict defendants accused of violent crimes than they are to convict defendants accused of "victimless" crimes or crimes against property.

GO ON TO THE NEXT PAGE.

24. Many major scientific discoveries of the past were the product of serendipity, the chance discovery of valuable findings that investigators had not purposely sought. Now, however, scientific research tends to be so costly that investigators are heavily dependent on large grants to fund their research. Because such grants require investigators to provide the grant sponsors with clear projections of the outcome of the proposed research, investigators ignore anything that does not directly bear on the funded research. Therefore, under the prevailing circumstances, serendipity can no longer play a role in scientific discovery.

Which one of the following is an assumption on which the argument depends?

(A) Only findings that an investigator purposely seeks can directly bear on that investigator's research.

(B) In the past few scientific investigators attempted to make clear predictions of the outcome of their research.

(C) Dependence on large grants is preventing investigators from conducting the type of scientific research that those investigators would personally prefer.

(D) All scientific investigators who provide grant sponsors with clear projections of the outcome of their research receive at least some of the grants for which they apply.

(E) In general the most valuable scientific discoveries are the product of serendipity.

25. Police statistics have shown that automobile antitheft devices reduce the risk of car theft, but a statistical study of automobile theft by the automobile insurance industry claims that cars equipped with antitheft devices are, paradoxically, more likely to be stolen than cars that are not so equipped.

Which one of the following, if true, does the most to resolve the apparent paradox?

(A) Owners of stolen cars almost invariably report the theft immediately to the police but tend to delay notifying their insurance company, in the hope that the vehicle will be recovered.

(B) Most cars that are stolen are not equipped with antitheft devices, and most cars that are equipped with antitheft devices are not stolen.

(C) The most common automobile antitheft devices are audible alarms, which typically produce ten false alarms for every actual attempted theft.

(D) Automobile owners who have particularly theft-prone cars and live in areas of greatest incidence of car theft are those who are most likely to have antitheft devices installed.

(E) Most automobile thefts are the work of professional thieves against whose efforts antitheft devices offer scant protection.

S T O P

IF YOU FINISH BEFORE TIME IS CALLED, YOU MAY CHECK YOUR WORK ON THIS SECTION ONLY.
DO NOT WORK ON ANY OTHER SECTION IN THE TEST.

SECTION II

Time—35 minutes

24 Questions

Directions: Each group of questions in this section is based on a set of conditions. In answering some of the questions, it may be useful to draw a rough diagram. Choose the response that most accurately and completely answers each question and blacken the corresponding space on your answer sheet.

Questions 1–7

Seven consecutive time slots for a broadcast, numbered in chronological order 1 through 7, will be filled by six song tapes—G, H, L, O, P, S—and exactly one news tape. Each tape is to be assigned to a different time slot, and no tape is longer than any other tape. The broadcast is subject to the following restrictions:

L must be played immediately before O.

The news tape must be played at some time after L.

There must be exactly two time slots between G and P, regardless of whether G comes before P or whether G comes after P.

1. If G is played second, which one of the following tapes must be played third?

   (A) the news
   (B) H
   (C) L
   (D) O
   (E) S

2. The news tape can be played in any one of the following time slots EXCEPT the

   (A) second
   (B) third
   (C) fourth
   (D) fifth
   (E) sixth

3. If H and S are to be scheduled as far from each other as possible, then the first, the second, and the third time slots could be filled, respectively, by

   (A) G, H, and L
   (B) S, G, and the news
   (C) H, G, and L
   (D) H, L, and O
   (E) L, O, and S

4. If P is played fifth, L must be played

   (A) first
   (B) second
   (C) third
   (D) fourth
   (E) sixth

5. What is the maximum number of tapes that can separate S from the news?

   (A) 1
   (B) 2
   (C) 3
   (D) 4
   (E) 5

6. Which one of the following is the latest time slot in which L can be played?

   (A) the third
   (B) the fourth
   (C) the fifth
   (D) the sixth
   (E) the seventh

7. The time slot in which O must be played is completely determined if G is assigned to which one of the following time slots?

   (A) the first
   (B) the third
   (C) the fourth
   (D) the fifth
   (E) the sixth

GO ON TO THE NEXT PAGE.

Questions 8–12

Doctor Yamata works only on Mondays, Tuesdays, Wednesdays, Fridays, and Saturdays. She performs four different activities—lecturing, operating, treating patients, and conducting research. Each working day she performs exactly one activity in the morning and exactly one activity in the afternoon. During each week her work schedule must satisfy the following restrictions:

She performs operations on exactly three mornings.

If she operates on Monday, she does not operate on Tuesday.

She lectures in the afternoon on exactly two consecutive calendar days.

She treats patients on exactly one morning and exactly three afternoons.

She conducts research on exactly one morning.

On Saturday she neither lectures nor performs operations.

8. Which one of the following must be a day on which Doctor Yamata lectures?

   (A) Monday
   (B) Tuesday
   (C) Wednesday
   (D) Friday
   (E) Saturday

9. On Wednesday Doctor Yamata could be scheduled to

   (A) conduct research in the morning and operate in the afternoon
   (B) lecture in the morning and treat patients in the afternoon
   (C) operate in the morning and lecture in the afternoon
   (D) operate in the morning and conduct research in the afternoon
   (E) treat patients in the morning and treat patients in the afternoon

10. Which one of the following statements must be true?

   (A) There is one day on which the doctor treats patients both in the morning and in the afternoon.
   (B) The doctor conducts research on one of the days on which she lectures.
   (C) The doctor conducts research on one of the days on which she treats patients.
   (D) The doctor lectures on one of the days on which she treats patients.
   (E) The doctor lectures on one of the days on which she operates.

11. If Doctor Yamata operates on Tuesday, then her schedule for treating patients could be

   (A) Monday morning, Monday afternoon, Friday morning, Friday afternoon
   (B) Monday morning, Friday afternoon, Saturday morning, Saturday afternoon
   (C) Monday afternoon, Wednesday morning, Wednesday afternoon, Saturday afternoon
   (D) Wednesday morning, Wednesday afternoon, Friday afternoon, Saturday afternoon
   (E) Wednesday afternoon, Friday afternoon, Saturday morning, Saturday afternoon

12. Which one of the following is a pair of days on both of which Doctor Yamata must treat patients?

   (A) Monday and Tuesday
   (B) Monday and Saturday
   (C) Tuesday and Friday
   (D) Tuesday and Saturday
   (E) Friday and Saturday

GO ON TO THE NEXT PAGE.

Questions 13–18

Each of seven judges voted for or else against granting Datalog Corporation's petition. Each judge is categorized as conservative, moderate, or liberal, and no judge is assigned more than one of those labels. Two judges are conservatives, two are moderates, and three are liberals. The following is known about how the judges voted:

If the two conservatives and at least one liberal voted the same way as each other, then both moderates voted that way.

If the three liberals voted the same way as each other, then no conservative voted that way.

At least two of the judges voted for Datalog, and at least two voted against Datalog.

At least one conservative voted against Datalog.

13. If the two moderates did not vote the same way as each other, then which one of the following could be true?

(A) No conservative and exactly two liberals voted for Datalog.
(B) Exactly one conservative and exactly one liberal voted for Datalog.
(C) Exactly one conservative and all three liberals voted for Datalog.
(D) Exactly two conservatives and exactly one liberal voted for Datalog.
(E) Exactly two conservatives and exactly two liberals voted for Datalog.

14. Which one of the following must be true?

(A) At least one conservative voted for Datalog.
(B) At least one liberal voted against Datalog.
(C) At least one liberal voted for Datalog.
(D) At least one moderate voted against Datalog.
(E) At least one moderate voted for Datalog.

15. If the three liberals all voted the same way as each other, which one of the following must be true?

(A) Both moderates voted for Datalog.
(B) Both moderates voted against Datalog.
(C) One conservative voted for Datalog and one conservative voted against Datalog.
(D) One moderate voted for Datalog and one moderate voted against Datalog.
(E) All three liberals voted for Datalog.

16. If exactly two judges voted against Datalog, then which one of the following must be true?

(A) Both moderates voted for Datalog.
(B) Exactly one conservative voted for Datalog.
(C) No conservative voted for Datalog.
(D) Exactly two liberals voted for Datalog.
(E) Exactly three liberals voted for Datalog.

17. Each of the following could be a complete and accurate list of those judges who voted for Datalog EXCEPT

(A) two liberals
(B) one conservative, one liberal
(C) two moderates, three liberals
(D) one conservative, two moderates, two liberals
(E) one conservative, two moderates, three liberals

18. If the two conservatives voted the same way as each other, but the liberals did not all vote the same way as each other, then each of the following must be true EXCEPT:

(A) Both conservatives voted against Datalog.
(B) Both moderates voted for Datalog.
(C) At least one liberal voted against Datalog.
(D) Exactly two liberals voted for Datalog.
(E) Exactly five of the judges voted against Datalog.

GO ON TO THE NEXT PAGE.

Questions 19–24

An official is assigning five runners—Larry, Ned, Olivia, Patricia, and Sonja—to parallel lanes numbered consecutively 1 through 5. The official will also assign each runner to represent a different charity—F, G, H, J, and K—not necessarily in order of the runner's names as given. The following ordering restrictions apply:

The runner representing K is assigned to lane 4.
Patricia is assigned to the only lane between the lanes of the runners representing F and G.
There are exactly two lanes between Olivia's lane and the lane of the runner representing G.
Sonja is assigned to a higher-numbered lane than the lane to which Ned is assigned.

19. Which one of the following is a possible assignment of runners to lanes by the charity they represent?

<u>1 2 3 4 5</u>
(A) F G H K J
(B) G H J K F
(C) G K F J H
(D) H J G K F
(E) J H F K G

20. The lane to which Patricia is assigned must be a lane that is

(A) next to the lane to which Larry is assigned
(B) next to the lane to which Ned is assigned
(C) separated by exactly one lane from the lane to which Ned is assigned
(D) separated by exactly one lane from the lane to which Olivia is assigned
(E) separated by exactly one lane from the lane to which Sonja is assigned

21. If Olivia is assigned to lane 2, which one of the following assignments must be made?

	Charity	Lane
(A)	F	1
(B)	G	5
(C)	H	1
(D)	H	3
(E)	J	5

22. Which one of the following is a complete and accurate list of runners each of whom could be the runner representing F?

(A) Larry, Ned
(B) Patricia, Sonja
(C) Larry, Ned, Olivia
(D) Larry, Ned, Sonja
(E) Ned, Patricia, Sonja

23. If Ned is the runner representing J, then it must be true that

(A) the runner representing G is assigned to lane 1
(B) the runner representing H is assigned to lane 2
(C) Larry is the runner representing K
(D) Olivia is the runner representing F
(E) Patricia is the runner representing H

24. If Larry represents J, which one of the following could be the assignment of runners to lanes?

	<u>1</u>	<u>2</u>	<u>3</u>	<u>4</u>	<u>5</u>
(A)	Larry	Olivia	Ned	Patricia	Sonja
(B)	Larry	Ned	Olivia	Sonja	Patricia
(C)	Larry	Sonja	Patricia	Ned	Olivia
(D)	Ned	Olivia	Larry	Patricia	Sonja
(E)	Ned	Sonja	Olivia	Patricia	Larry

S T O P

IF YOU FINISH BEFORE TIME IS CALLED, YOU MAY CHECK YOUR WORK ON THIS SECTION ONLY.
DO NOT WORK ON ANY OTHER SECTION IN THE TEST.

SECTION III

Time—35 minutes

27 Questions

Directions: Each passage in this section is followed by a group of questions to be answered on the basis of what is stated or implied in the passage. For some of the questions, more than one of the choices could conceivably answer the question. However, you are to choose the best answer; that is, the response that most accurately and completely answers the question, and blacken the corresponding space on your answer sheet.

The labor force is often organized as if workers had no family responsibilities. Preschool-age children need full-time care; children in primary school need care after school and during school
(5) vacations. Although day-care services can resolve some scheduling conflicts between home and office, workers cannot always find or afford suitable care. Even when they obtain such care, parents must still cope with emergencies, such as illnesses, that keep
(10) children at home. Moreover, children need more than tending; they also need meaningful time with their parents. Conventional full-time workdays, especially when combined with unavoidable household duties, are too inflexible for parents
(15) with primary child-care responsibility.

Although a small but increasing number of working men are single parents, those barriers against successful participation in the labor market that are related to primary child-care
(20) responsibilities mainly disadvantage women. Even in families where both parents work, cultural pressures are traditionally much greater on mothers than on fathers to bear the primary child-rearing responsibilities.

(25) In reconciling child-rearing responsibilities with participation in the labor market, many working mothers are forced to make compromises. For example, approximately one-third of all working mothers are employed only part-time, even though
(30) part-time jobs are dramatically underpaid and often less desirable in comparison to full-time employment. Even though part-time work is usually available only in occupations offering minimal employee responsibility and little
(35) opportunity for advancement or self-enrichment, such employment does allow many women the time and flexibility to fulfill their family duties, but only at the expense of the advantages associated with full-time employment.

(40) Moreover, even mothers with full-time employment must compromise opportunities in order to adjust to barriers against parents in the labor market. Many choose jobs entailing little challenge or responsibility or those offering flexible
(45) scheduling, often available only in poorly paid positions, while other working mothers, although willing and able to assume as much responsibility as people without children, find that their need to spend regular and predictable time with their
(50) children inevitably causes them to lose career

opportunities to those without such demands. Thus, women in education are more likely to become teachers than school administrators, whose more conventional full-time work schedules do not
(55) correspond to the schedules of school-age children, while female lawyers are more likely to practice law in trusts and estates, where they can control their work schedules, than in litigation, where they cannot. Nonprofessional women are concentrated
(60) in secretarial work and department store sales, where their absences can be covered easily by substitutes and where they can enter and leave the work force with little loss, since the jobs offer so little personal gain. Indeed, as long as the labor
(65) market remains hostile to parents, and family roles continue to be allocated on the basis of gender, women will be seriously disadvantaged in that labor market.

1. Which one of the following best summarizes the main idea of the passage?

(A) Current trends in the labor force indicate that working parents, especially women, may not always need to choose between occupational and child-care responsibilities.
(B) In order for mothers to have an equal opportunity for advancement in the labor force, traditional family roles have to be reexamined and revised.
(C) Although single parents who work have to balance parental and career demands, single mothers suffer resulting employment disadvantages that single fathers can almost always avoid.
(D) Although child-care responsibilities disadvantage many women in the labor force, professional women (such as teachers and lawyers) are better able to overcome this problem than are nonprofessional women.
(E) Traditional work schedules are too inflexible to accommodate the child-care responsibilities of many parents, a fact that severely disadvantages women in the labor force.

GO ON TO THE NEXT PAGE.

2. Which one of the following statements about part-time work can be inferred from the information presented in the passage?

   (A) One-third of all part-time workers are working mothers.
   (B) Part-time work generally offers fewer opportunities for advancement to working mothers than to women generally.
   (C) Part-time work, in addition to having relatively poor wages, often requires that employees work during holidays, when their children are out of school.
   (D) Part-time employment, despite its disadvantages, provides working mothers with an opportunity to address some of the demands of caring for children.
   (E) Many mothers with primary child-care responsibility choose part-time jobs in order to better exploit full-time career opportunities after their children are grown.

3. It can be inferred from the passage that the author would be most likely to agree with which one of the following statements about working fathers in two-parent families?

   (A) They are equally burdened by the employment disadvantages placed upon all parents—male and female—in the labor market.
   (B) They are so absorbed in their jobs that they often do not see the injustice going on around them.
   (C) They are shielded by the traditional allocation of family roles from many of the pressures associated with child-rearing responsibilities.
   (D) They help compound the inequities in the labor market by keeping women from competing with men for career opportunities.
   (E) They are responsible for many of the problems of working mothers because of their insistence on traditional roles in the family.

4. Of the following, which one would the author most likely say is the most troublesome barrier facing working parents with primary child-care responsibility?

   (A) the lack of full-time jobs open to women
   (B) the inflexibility of work schedules
   (C) the low wages of part-time employment
   (D) the limited advancement opportunities for nonprofessional employees
   (E) the practice of allocating responsibilities in the workplace on the basis of gender

5. The passage suggests that day care is at best a limited solution to the pressures associated with child rearing for all of the following reasons EXCEPT:

   (A) Even the best day care available cannot guarantee that children will have meaningful time with their parents.
   (B) Some parents cannot afford day-care services.
   (C) Working parents sometimes have difficulty finding suitable day care for their children.
   (D) Parents who send their children to day care still need to provide care for their children during vacations.
   (E) Even children who are in day care may have to stay home when they are sick.

6. According to the passage, many working parents may be forced to make any of the following types of career decisions EXCEPT

   (A) declining professional positions for nonprofessional ones, which typically have less conventional work schedules
   (B) accepting part-time employment rather than full-time employment
   (C) taking jobs with limited responsibility, and thus more limited career opportunities, in order to have a more flexible schedule
   (D) pursuing career specializations that allow them to control their work schedules instead of pursuing a more desirable specialization in the same field
   (E) limiting the career potential of one parent, often the mother, who assumes greater child-care responsibility

7. Which one of the following statements would most appropriately continue the discussion at the end of the passage?

   (A) At the same time, most men will remain better able to enjoy the career and salary opportunities offered by the labor market.
   (B) Of course, men who are married to working mothers know of these employment barriers but seem unwilling to do anything about them.
   (C) On the other hand, salary levels may become more equitable between men and women even if the other career opportunities remain more accessible to men than to women.
   (D) On the contrary, men with primary child-rearing responsibilities will continue to enjoy more advantages in the workplace than their female counterparts.
   (E) Thus, institutions in society that favor men over women will continue to widen the gap between the career opportunities available for men and for women.

Critics have long been puzzled by the inner contradictions of major characters in John Webster's tragedies. In his *The Duchess of Malfi*, for instance, the Duchess is "good" in demonstrating (5) the obvious tenderness and sincerity of her love for Antonio, but "bad" in ignoring the wishes and welfare of her family and in making religion a "cloak" hiding worldly self-indulgence. Bosola is "bad" in serving Ferdinand, "good" in turning the (10) Duchess' thoughts toward heaven and in planning to avenge her murder. The ancient Greek philosopher Aristotle implied that such contradictions are virtually essential to the tragic personality, and yet critics keep coming back to this element of (15) inconsistency as though it were an eccentric feature of Webster's own tragic vision.

The problem is that, as an Elizabethan playwright, Webster has become a prisoner of our critical presuppositions. We have, in recent years, been (20) dazzled by the way the earlier Renaissance and medieval theater, particularly the morality play, illuminates Elizabethan drama. We now understand how the habit of mind that saw the world as a battleground between good and evil produced the (25) morality play. Morality plays allegorized that conflict by presenting characters whose actions were defined as the embodiment of good or evil. This model of reality lived on, overlaid by different conventions, in the more sophisticated Elizabethan (30) works of the following age. Yet Webster seems not to have been as heavily influenced by the morality play's model of reality as were his Elizabethan contemporaries; he was apparently more sensitive to the more morally complicated Italian drama (35) than to these English sources. Consequently, his characters cannot be evaluated according to reductive formulas of good and evil, which is precisely what modern critics have tried to do. They choose what seem to be the most promising of the (40) contradictory values that are dramatized in the play, and treat those values as if they were the only basis for analyzing the moral development of the play's major characters, attributing the inconsistencies in a character's behavior to artistic (45) incompetence on Webster's part. The lack of consistency in Webster's characters can be better understood if we recognize that the ambiguity at the heart of his tragic vision lies not in the external world but in the duality of human nature. Webster (50) establishes tension in his plays by setting up conflicting systems of value that appear immoral only when one value system is viewed exclusively from the perspective of the other. He presents us not only with characters that we condemn (55) intellectually or ethically and at the same time impulsively approve of, but also with judgments we must accept as logically sound and yet find emotionally repulsive. The dilemma is not only dramatic: it is tragic, because the conflict is (60) irreconcilable, and because it is ours as much as that of the characters.

8. The primary purpose of the passage is to

(A) clarify an ambiguous assertion
(B) provide evidence in support of a commonly held view
(C) analyze an unresolved question and propose an answer
(D) offer an alternative to a flawed interpretation
(E) describe and categorize opposing viewpoints

9. The author suggests which one of the following about the dramatic works that most influenced Webster's tragedies?

(A) They were not concerned with dramatizing the conflict between good and evil that was presented in morality plays.
(B) They were not as sophisticated as the Italian sources from which other Elizabethan tragedies were derived.
(C) They have never been adequately understood by critics.
(D) They have only recently been used to illuminate the conventions of Elizabethan drama.
(E) They have been considered by many critics to be the reason for Webster's apparent artistic incompetence.

10. The author's allusion to Aristotle's view of tragedy in lines 11–13 serves which one of the following functions in the passage?

(A) It introduces a commonly held view of Webster's tragedies that the author plans to defend.
(B) It supports the author's suggestion that Webster's conception of tragedy is not idiosyncratic.
(C) It provides an example of an approach to Webster's tragedies that the author criticizes.
(D) It establishes the similarity between classical and modern approaches to tragedy.
(E) It supports the author's assertion that Elizabethan tragedy cannot be fully understood without the help of recent scholarship.

GO ON TO THE NEXT PAGE.

11. It can be inferred from the passage that modern critics' interpretations of Webster's tragedies would be more valid if

   (A) the ambiguity inherent in Webster's tragic vision resulted from the duality of human nature
   (B) Webster's conception of the tragic personality were similar to that of Aristotle
   (C) Webster had been heavily influenced by the morality play
   (D) Elizabethan dramatists had been more sensitive to Italian sources of influence
   (E) the inner conflicts exhibited by Webster's characters were similar to those of modern audiences

12. With which one of the following statements regarding Elizabethan drama would the author be most likely to agree?

   (A) The skill of Elizabethan dramatists has in recent years been overestimated.
   (B) The conventions that shaped Elizabethan drama are best exemplified by Webster's drama.
   (C) Elizabethan drama, for the most part, can be viewed as being heavily influenced by the morality play.
   (D) Only by carefully examining the work of his Elizabethan contemporaries can Webster's achievement as a dramatist be accurately measured.
   (E) Elizabethan drama can best be described as influenced by a composite of Italian and classical sources.

13. It can be inferred from the passage that most modern critics assume which one of the following in their interpretation of Webster's tragedies?

   (A) Webster's plays tended to allegorize the conflict between good and evil more than did those of his contemporaries.
   (B) Webster's plays were derived more from Italian than from English sources.
   (C) The artistic flaws in Webster's tragedies were largely the result of his ignorance of the classical definition of tragedy.
   (D) Webster's tragedies provide no relevant basis for analyzing the moral development of their characters.
   (E) In writing his tragedies, Webster was influenced by the same sources as his contemporaries.

14. The author implies that Webster's conception of tragedy was

   (A) artistically flawed
   (B) highly conventional
   (C) largely derived from the morality play
   (D) somewhat different from the conventional Elizabethan conception of tragedy
   (E) uninfluenced by the classical conception of tragedy

GO ON TO THE NEXT PAGE.

Cultivation of a single crop on a given tract of land leads eventually to decreased yields. One reason for this is that harmful bacterial phytopathogens, organisms parasitic on plant
(5) hosts, increase in the soil surrounding plant roots. The problem can be cured by crop rotation, denying the pathogens a suitable host for a period of time. However, even if crops are not rotated, the severity of diseases brought on by such
(10) phytopathogens often decreases after a number of years as the microbial population of the soil changes and the soil becomes "suppressive" to those diseases. While there may be many reasons for this phenomenon, it is clear that levels of certain
(15) bacteria, such as *Pseudomonas fluorescens*, a bacterium antagonistic to a number of harmful phytopathogens, are greater in suppressive than in nonsuppressive soil. This suggests that the presence of such bacteria suppresses phytopathogens. There
(20) is now considerable experimental support for this view. Wheat yield increases of 27 percent have been obtained in field trials by treatment of wheat seeds with fluorescent pseudomonads. Similar treatment of sugar beets, cotton, and potatoes has had similar
(25) results.

These improvements in crop yields through the application of *Pseudomonas fluorescens* suggest that agriculture could benefit from the use of bacteria genetically altered for specific purposes. For
(30) example, a form of phytopathogen altered to remove its harmful properties could be released into the environment in quantities favorable to its competing with and eventually excluding the harmful normal strain. Some experiments suggest
(35) that deliberately releasing altered nonpathogenic *Pseudomonas syringae* could crowd out the nonaltered variety that causes frost damage. Opponents of such research have objected that the deliberate and large-scale release of genetically
(40) altered bacteria might have deleterious results. Proponents, on the other hand, argue that this particular strain is altered only by the removal of the gene responsible for the strain's propensity to cause frost damage, thereby rendering it safer than
(45) the phytopathogen from which it was derived.

Some proponents have gone further and suggest that genetic alteration techniques could create organisms with totally new combinations of desirable traits not found in nature. For example,
(50) genes responsible for production of insecticidal compounds have been transposed from other bacteria into pseudomonads that colonize corn roots. Experiments of this kind are difficult and require great care: such bacteria are developed in
(55) highly artificial environments and may not compete well with natural soil bacteria. Nevertheless, proponents contend that the prospects for improved agriculture through such methods seem excellent. These prospects lead many to hope that
(60) current efforts to assess the risks of deliberate

release of altered microorganisms will successfully answer the concerns of opponents and create a climate in which such research can go forward without undue impediment.

15. Which one of the following best summarizes the main idea of the passage?

(A) Recent field experiments with genetically altered *Pseudomonas* bacteria have shown that releasing genetically altered bacteria into the environment would not involve any significant danger.
(B) Encouraged by current research, advocates of agricultural use of genetically altered bacteria are optimistic that such use will eventually result in improved agriculture, though opponents remain wary.
(C) Current research indicates that adding genetically altered *Pseudomonas syringae* bacteria to the soil surrounding crop plant roots will have many beneficial effects, such as the prevention of frost damage in certain crops.
(D) Genetic alteration of a number of harmful phytopathogens has been advocated by many researchers who contend that these techniques will eventually replace such outdated methods as crop rotation.
(E) Genetic alteration of bacteria has been successful in highly artificial laboratory conditions, but opponents of such research have argued that these techniques are unlikely to produce organisms that are able to survive in natural environments.

16. The author discusses naturally occurring *Pseudomonas fluorescens* bacteria in the first paragraph primarily in order to do which one of the following?

(A) prove that increases in the level of such bacteria in the soil are the sole cause of soil suppressivity
(B) explain why yields increased after wheat fields were sprayed with altered *Pseudomonas fluorescens* bacteria
(C) detail the chemical processes that such bacteria use to suppress organisms parasitic to crop plants, such as wheat, sugar beets, and potatoes
(D) provide background information to support the argument that research into the agricultural use of genetically altered bacteria would be fruitful
(E) argue that crop rotation is unnecessary, since diseases brought on by phytopathogens diminish in severity and eventually disappear on their own

GO ON TO THE NEXT PAGE.

17. It can be inferred from the author's discussion of *Pseudomonas fluorescens* bacteria that which one of the following would be true of crops impervious to parasitical organisms?

    (A) *Pseudomonas fluorescens* bacteria would be absent from the soil surrounding their roots.
    (B) They would crowd out and eventually exclude other crop plants if their growth were not carefully regulated.
    (C) Their yield would not be likely to be improved by adding *Pseudomonas fluorescens* bacteria to the soil.
    (D) They would mature more quickly than crop plants that were susceptible to parasitical organisms.
    (E) Levels of phytopathogenic bacteria in the soil surrounding their roots would be higher compared with other crop plants.

18. It can be inferred from the passage that crop rotation can increase yields in part because

    (A) moving crop plants around makes them hardier and more resistant to disease
    (B) the number of *Pseudomonas fluorescens* bacteria in the soil usually increases when crops are rotated
    (C) the roots of many crop plants produce compounds that are antagonistic to phytopathogens harmful to other crop plants
    (D) the presence of phytopathogenic bacteria is responsible for the majority of plant diseases
    (E) phytopathogens typically attack some plant species but find other species to be unsuitable hosts

19. According to the passage, proponents of the use of genetically altered bacteria in agriculture argue that which one of the following is true of the altered bacteria used in the frost-damage experiments?

    (A) The altered bacteria had a genetic constitution differing from that of the normal strain only in that the altered variety had one less gene.
    (B) Although the altered bacteria competed effectively with the nonaltered strain in the laboratory, they were not as viable in natural environments.
    (C) The altered bacteria were much safer and more effective than the naturally occurring *Pseudomonas fluorescens* bacteria used in earlier experiments.
    (D) The altered bacteria were antagonistic to several types of naturally occurring phytopathogens in the soil surrounding the roots of frost-damaged crops.
    (E) The altered bacteria were released into the environment in numbers sufficient to guarantee the validity of experimental results.

20. Which one of the following, if true, would most seriously weaken the proponents' argument regarding the safety of using altered *Pseudomonas syringae* bacteria to control frost damage?

    (A) *Pseudomonas syringae* bacteria are primitive and have a simple genetic constitution.
    (B) The altered bacteria are derived from a strain that is parasitic to plants and can cause damage to crops.
    (C) Current genetic-engineering techniques permit the large-scale commercial production of such bacteria.
    (D) Often genes whose presence is responsible for one harmful characteristic must be present in order to prevent other harmful characteristics.
    (E) The frost-damage experiments with *Pseudomonas syringae* bacteria indicate that the altered variety would only replace the normal strain if released in sufficient numbers.

GO ON TO THE NEXT PAGE.

In 1887 the Dawes Act legislated wide-scale private ownership of reservation lands in the United States for Native Americans. The act allotted plots of 80 acres to each Native American
(5) adult. However, the Native Americans were not granted outright title to their lands. The act defined each grant as a "trust patent," meaning that the Bureau of Indian Affairs (BIA), the governmental agency in charge of administering policy regarding
(10) Native Americans, would hold the allotted land in trust for 25 years, during which time the Native American owners could use, but not alienate (sell) the land. After the 25-year period, the Native American allottee would receive a "fee patent"
(15) awarding full legal ownership of the land.

Two main reasons were advanced for the restriction on the Native Americans' ability to sell their lands. First, it was claimed that free alienability would lead to immediate transfer of
(20) large amounts of former reservation land to non-Native Americans, consequently threatening the traditional way of life on those reservations. A second objection to free alienation was that Native Americans were unaccustomed to, and did not
(25) desire, a system of private landownership. Their custom, it was said, favored communal use of land.

However, both of these arguments bear only on the transfer of Native American lands to non-Native Americans; neither offers a reason for prohibiting
(30) Native Americans from transferring land among themselves. Selling land to each other would not threaten the Native American culture. Additionally, if communal land use remained preferable to Native Americans after allotment, free
(35) alienability would have allowed allottees to sell their lands back to the tribe.

When stated rationales for government policies prove empty, using an interest-group model often provides an explanation. While neither Native
(40) Americans nor the potential non-Native American purchasers benefited from the restraint on alienation contained in the Dawes Act, one clearly defined group did benefit: the BIA bureaucrats. It has been convincingly demonstrated that bureaucrats
(45) seek to maximize the size of their staffs and their budgets in order to compensate for the lack of other sources of fulfillment, such as power and prestige. Additionally, politicians tend to favor the growth of governmental bureaucracy because such
(50) growth provides increased opportunity for the exercise of political patronage. The restraint on alienation vastly increased the amount of work, and hence the budgets, necessary to implement the statute. Until allotment was ended in 1934,
(55) granting fee patents and leasing Native American lands were among the principal activities of the United States government. One hypothesis, then, for the temporary restriction on alienation in the Dawes Act is that it reflected a compromise
(60) between non-Native Americans favoring immediate alienability so they could purchase land and the BIA bureaucrats who administered the privatization system.

21. Which one of the following best summarizes the main idea of the passage?

(A) United States government policy toward Native Americans has tended to disregard their needs and consider instead the needs of non-Native American purchasers of land.

(B) In order to preserve the unique way of life on Native American reservations, use of Native American lands must be communal rather than individual.

(C) The Dawes Act's restriction on the right of Native Americans to sell their land may have been implemented primarily to serve the interests of politicians and bureaucrats.

(D) The clause restricting free alienability in the Dawes Act greatly expanded United States governmental activity in the area of land administration.

(E) Since passage of the Dawes Act in 1887, Native Americans have not been able to sell or transfer their former reservation land freely.

22. Which one of the following statements concerning the reason for the end of allotment, if true, would provide the most support for the author's view of politicians?

(A) Politicians realized that allotment was damaging the Native American way of life.

(B) Politicians decided that allotment would be more congruent with the Native American custom of communal land use.

(C) Politicians believed that allotment's continuation would not enhance their opportunities to exercise patronage.

(D) Politicians felt that the staff and budgets of the BIA had grown too large.

(E) Politicians were concerned that too much Native American land was falling into the hands of non-Native Americans.

GO ON TO THE NEXT PAGE.

23. Which one of the following best describes the organization of the passage?

   (A) The passage of a law is analyzed in detail, the benefits and drawbacks of one of its clauses are studied, and a final assessment of the law is offered.
   (B) The history of a law is narrated, the effects of one of its clauses on various populations are studied, and repeal of the law is advocated.
   (C) A law is examined, the political and social backgrounds of one of its clauses are characterized, and the permanent effects of the law are studied.
   (D) A law is described, the rationale put forward for one of its clauses is outlined and dismissed, and a different rationale for the clause is presented.
   (E) The legal status of an ethnic group is examined with respect to issues of landownership and commercial autonomy, and the benefits to rival groups due to that status are explained.

24. The author's attitude toward the reasons advanced for the restriction on alienability in the Dawes Act at the time of its passage can best be described as

   (A) completely credulous
   (B) partially approving
   (C) basically indecisive
   (D) mildly questioning
   (E) highly skeptical

25. It can be inferred from the passage that which one of the following was true of Native American life immediately before passage of the Dawes Act?

   (A) Most Native Americans supported themselves through farming.
   (B) Not many Native Americans personally owned the land on which they lived.
   (C) The land on which most Native Americans lived had been bought from their tribes.
   (D) Few Native Americans had much contact with their non-Native American neighbors.
   (E) Few Native Americans were willing to sell their land to non-Native Americans.

26. According to the passage, the type of landownership initially obtainable by Native Americans under the Dawes Act differed from the type of ownership obtainable after a 25-year period in that only the latter allowed

   (A) owners of land to farm it
   (B) owners of land to sell it
   (C) government some control over how owners disposed of land
   (D) owners of land to build on it with relatively minor governmental restrictions
   (E) government to charge owners a fee for developing their land

27. Which one of the following, if true, would most strengthen the author's argument regarding the true motivation for the passage of the Dawes Act?

   (A) The legislators who voted in favor of the Dawes Act owned land adjacent to Native American reservations.
   (B) The majority of Native Americans who were granted fee patents did not sell their land back to their tribes.
   (C) Native Americans managed to preserve their traditional culture even when they were geographically dispersed.
   (D) The legislators who voted in favor of the Dawes Act were heavily influenced by BIA bureaucrats.
   (E) Non-Native Americans who purchased the majority of Native American lands consolidated them into larger farm holdings.

S T O P

IF YOU FINISH BEFORE TIME IS CALLED, YOU MAY CHECK YOUR WORK ON THIS SECTION ONLY.
DO NOT WORK ON ANY OTHER SECTION IN THE TEST.

SECTION IV

Time—35 minutes

25 Questions

Directions: The questions in this section are based on the reasoning contained in brief statements or passages. For some questions, more than one of the choices could conceivably answer the question. However, you are to choose the best answer; that is, the response that most accurately and completely answers the question. You should not make assumptions that are by commonsense standards implausible, superfluous, or incompatible with the passage. After you have chosen the best answer, blacken the corresponding space on your answer sheet.

1. In 1974 the speed limit on highways in the United States was reduced to 55 miles per hour in order to save fuel. In the first 12 months after the change, the rate of highway fatalities dropped 15 percent, the sharpest one-year drop in history. Over the next 10 years, the fatality rate declined by another 25 percent. It follows that the 1974 reduction in the speed limit saved many lives.

Which one of the following, if true, most strengthens the argument?

(A) The 1974 fuel shortage cut driving sharply for more than a year.

(B) There was no decline in the rate of highway fatalities during the twelfth year following the reduction in the speed limit.

(C) Since 1974 automobile manufacturers have been required by law to install lifesaving equipment, such as seat belts, in all new cars.

(D) The fatality rate in highway accidents involving motorists driving faster than 55 miles per hour is much higher than in highway accidents that do not involve motorists driving at such speeds.

(E) Motorists are more likely to avoid accidents by matching their speed to that of the surrounding highway traffic than by driving at faster or slower speeds.

2. Some legislators refuse to commit public funds for new scientific research if they cannot be assured that the research will contribute to the public welfare. Such a position ignores the lessons of experience. Many important contributions to the public welfare that resulted from scientific research were never predicted as potential outcomes of that research. Suppose that a scientist in the early twentieth century had applied for public funds to study molds: who would have predicted that such research would lead to the discovery of antibiotics—one of the greatest contributions ever made to the public welfare?

Which one of the following most accurately expresses the main point of the argument?

(A) The committal of public funds for new scientific research will ensure that the public welfare will be enhanced.

(B) If it were possible to predict the general outcome of a new scientific research effort, then legislators would not refuse to commit public funds for that effort.

(C) Scientific discoveries that have contributed to the public welfare would have occurred sooner if public funds had been committed to the research that generated those discoveries.

(D) In order to ensure that scientific research is directed toward contributing to the public welfare, legislators must commit public funds to new scientific research.

(E) Lack of guarantees that new scientific research will contribute to the public welfare is not sufficient reason for legislators to refuse to commit public funds to new scientific research.

GO ON TO THE NEXT PAGE.

3. When workers do not find their assignments challenging, they become bored and so achieve less than their abilities would allow. On the other hand, when workers find their assignments too difficult, they give up and so again achieve less than what they are capable of achieving. It is, therefore, clear that no worker's full potential will ever be realized.

Which one of the following is an error of reasoning contained in the argument?

(A) mistakenly equating what is actual and what is merely possible
(B) assuming without warrant that a situation allows only two possibilities
(C) relying on subjective rather than objective evidence
(D) confusing the coincidence of two events with a causal relation between the two
(E) depending on the ambiguous use of a key term

4. Our tomato soup provides good nutrition: for instance, a warm bowl of it contains more units of vitamin C than does a serving of apricots or fresh carrots!

The advertisement is misleading if which one of the following is true?

(A) Few people depend exclusively on apricots and carrots to supply vitamin C to their diets.
(B) A liquid can lose vitamins if it stands in contact with the air for a protracted period of time.
(C) Tomato soup contains important nutrients other than vitamin C.
(D) The amount of vitamin C provided by a serving of the advertised soup is less than the amount furnished by a serving of fresh strawberries.
(E) Apricots and fresh carrots are widely known to be nutritious, but their contribution consists primarily in providing a large amount of vitamin A, not a large amount of vitamin C.

Questions 5–6

The government provides insurance for individuals' bank deposits, but requires the banks to pay the premiums for this insurance. Since it is depositors who primarily benefit from the security this insurance provides, the government should take steps to ensure that depositors who want this security bear the cost of it and thus should make depositors pay the premiums for insuring their own accounts.

5. Which one of the following principles, if established, would do most to justify drawing the conclusion of the argument on the basis of the reasons offered in its support?

(A) The people who stand to benefit from an economic service should always be made to bear the costs of that service.
(B) Any rational system of insurance must base the size of premiums on the degree of risk involved.
(C) Government-backed security for investors, such as bank depositors, should be provided only when it does not reduce incentives for investors to make responsible investments.
(D) The choice of not accepting an offered service should always be available, even if there is no charge for the service.
(E) The government should avoid any actions that might alter the behavior of corporations and individuals in the market.

6. Which one of the following is assumed by the argument?

(A) Banks are not insured by the government against default on the loans the banks make.
(B) Private insurance companies do not have the resources to provide banks or individuals with deposit insurance.
(C) Banks do not always cover the cost of the deposit-insurance premiums by paying depositors lower interest rates on insured deposits than the banks would on uninsured deposits.
(D) The government limits the insurance protection it provides by insuring accounts up to a certain legally defined amount only.
(E) The government does not allow banks to offer some kinds of accounts in which deposits are not insured.

GO ON TO THE NEXT PAGE.

7. When individual students are all treated equally in that they have identical exposure to curriculum material, the rate, quality, and quantity of learning will vary from student to student. If all students are to master a given curriculum, some of them need different types of help than others, as any experienced teacher knows.

If the statements above are both true, which one of the following conclusions can be drawn on the basis of them?

(A) Unequal treatment, in a sense, of individual students is required in order to ensure equality with respect to the educational tasks they master.
(B) The rate and quality of learning, with learning understood as the acquiring of the ability to solve problems within a given curriculum area, depend on the quantity of teaching an individual student receives in any given curriculum.
(C) The more experienced the teacher is, the more the students will learn.
(D) All students should have identical exposure to learn the material being taught in any given curriculum.
(E) Teachers should help each of their students to learn as much as possible.

8. George: Some scientists say that global warming will occur because people are releasing large amounts of carbon dioxide into the atmosphere by burning trees and fossil fuels. We can see, though, that the predicted warming is occurring already. In the middle of last winter, we had a month of springlike weather in our area, and this fall, because of unusually mild temperatures, the leaves on our town's trees were three weeks late in turning color.

Which one of the following would it be most relevant to investigate in evaluating the conclusion of George's argument?

(A) whether carbon dioxide is the only cause of global warming
(B) when leaves on the trees in the town usually change color
(C) what proportion of global emissions of carbon dioxide is due to the burning of trees by humans
(D) whether air pollution is causing some trees in the area to lose their leaves
(E) whether unusually warm weather is occurring elsewhere on the globe more frequently than before

9. Student representative: Our university, in expelling a student who verbally harassed his roommate, has erred by penalizing the student for doing what he surely has a right to do: speak his mind!
Dean of students: But what you're saying is that our university should endorse verbal harassment. Yet surely if we did that, we would threaten the free flow of ideas that is the essence of university life.

Which one of the following is a questionable technique that the dean of students uses in attempting to refute the student representative?

(A) challenging the student representative's knowledge of the process by which the student was expelled
(B) invoking a fallacious distinction between speech and other sorts of behavior
(C) misdescribing the student representative's position, thereby making it easier to challenge
(D) questioning the motives of the student representative rather than offering reasons for the conclusion defended
(E) relying on a position of power to silence the opposing viewpoint with a threat

10. Famous personalities found guilty of many types of crimes in well-publicized trials are increasingly sentenced to the performance of community service, though unknown defendants convicted of similar crimes almost always serve prison sentences. However, the principle of equality before the law rules out using fame and publicity as relevant considerations in the sentencing of convicted criminals.

The statements above, if true, most strongly support which one of the following conclusions?

(A) The principle of equality before the law is rigorously applied in only a few types of criminal trials.
(B) The number of convicted celebrities sentenced to community service should equal the number of convicted unknown defendants sentenced to community service.
(C) The principle of equality before the law can properly be overridden by other principles in some cases.
(D) The sentencing of celebrities to community service instead of prison constitutes a violation of the principle of equality before the law in many cases.
(E) The principle of equality before the law does not allow for leniency in sentencing.

GO ON TO THE NEXT PAGE.

11. Scientific research at a certain university was supported in part by an annual grant from a major foundation. When the university's physics department embarked on weapons-related research, the foundation, which has a purely humanitarian mission, threatened to cancel its grant. The university then promised that none of the foundation's money would be used for the weapons research, whereupon the foundation withdrew its threat, concluding that the weapons research would not benefit from the foundation's grant.

Which one of the following describes a flaw in the reasoning underlying the foundation's conclusion?

(A) It overlooks the possibility that the availability of the foundation's money for humanitarian uses will allow the university to redirect other funds from humanitarian uses to weapons research.

(B) It overlooks the possibility that the physics department's weapons research is not the only one of the university's research activities with other than purely humanitarian purposes.

(C) It overlooks the possibility that the university made its promise specifically in order to induce the foundation to withdraw its threat.

(D) It confuses the intention of not using a sum of money for a particular purpose with the intention of not using that sum of money at all.

(E) It assumes that if the means to achieve an objective are humanitarian in character, then the objective is also humanitarian in character.

12. To suit the needs of corporate clients, advertising agencies have successfully modified a strategy originally developed for political campaigns. This strategy aims to provide clients with free publicity and air time by designing an advertising campaign that is controversial, thus drawing prime-time media coverage and evoking public comment by officials.

The statements above, if true, most seriously undermine which one of the following assertions?

(A) The usefulness of an advertising campaign is based solely on the degree to which the campaign's advertisements persuade their audiences.

(B) Only a small percentage of eligible voters admit to being influenced by advertising campaigns in deciding how to vote.

(C) Campaign managers have transformed political campaigns by making increasing use of strategies borrowed from corporate advertising campaigns.

(D) Corporations are typically more concerned with maintaining public recognition of the corporate name than with enhancing goodwill toward the corporation.

(E) Advertising agencies that specialize in campaigns for corporate clients are not usually chosen for political campaigns.

13. The National Association of Fire Fighters says that 45 percent of homes now have smoke detectors, whereas only 30 percent of homes had them 10 years ago. This makes early detection of house fires no more likely, however, because over half of the domestic smoke detectors are either without batteries or else inoperative for some other reason.

In order for the conclusion above to be properly drawn, which one of the following assumptions would have to be made?

(A) Fifteen percent of domestic smoke detectors were installed less than 10 years ago.

(B) The number of fires per year in homes with smoke detectors has increased.

(C) Not all of the smoke detectors in homes are battery operated.

(D) The proportion of domestic smoke detectors that are inoperative has increased in the past ten years.

(E) Unlike automatic water sprinklers, a properly functioning smoke detector cannot by itself increase fire safety in a home.

GO ON TO THE NEXT PAGE.

14. Advertisement: HomeGlo Paints, Inc., has won the prestigious Golden Paintbrush Award—given to the one paint manufacturer in the country that has increased the environmental safety of its product most over the past three years— for HomeGlo Exterior Enamel. The Golden Paintbrush is awarded only on the basis of thorough tests by independent testing laboratories. So when you choose HomeGlo Exterior Enamel, you will know that you have chosen the most environmentally safe brand of paint manufactured in this country today.

The flawed reasoning in the advertisement most closely parallels that in which one of the following?

(A) The ZXC audio system received the overall top ranking for looks, performance, durability, and value in *Listeners' Report* magazine's ratings of currently produced systems. Therefore, the ZXC must have better sound quality than any other currently produced sound system.

(B) Morning Sunshine breakfast cereal contains, ounce for ounce, more of the nutrients needed for a healthy diet than any other breakfast cereal on the market today. Thus, when you eat Morning Sunshine, you will know you are eating the most nutritious food now on the market.

(C) The number of consumer visits increased more at Countryside Market last year than at any other market in the region. Therefore, Countryside's profits must also have increased more last year than those of any other market in the region.

(D) Jerrold's teachers recognize him as the student who has shown more academic improvement than any other student in the junior class this year. Therefore, if Jerrold and his classmates are ranked according to their current academic performance, Jerrold must hold the highest ranking.

(E) Margaret Durring's short story "The Power Lunch" won three separate awards for best short fiction of the year. Therefore, any of Margaret Durring's earlier stories certainly has enough literary merit to be included in an anthology of the best recent short fiction.

15. The consistency of ice cream is adversely affected by even slight temperature changes in the freezer. To counteract this problem, manufacturers add stabilizers to ice cream. Unfortunately, stabilizers, though inexpensive, adversely affect flavor. Stabilizers are less needed if storage temperatures are very low. However, since energy costs are constantly going up, those costs constitute a strong incentive in favor of relatively high storage temperatures.

Which one of the following can be properly inferred from the passage?

(A) Even slight deviations from the proper consistency for ice cream sharply impair its flavor.

(B) Cost considerations favor sacrificing consistency over sacrificing flavor.

(C) It would not be cost-effective to develop a new device to maintain the constancy of freezer temperatures.

(D) Stabilizers function well only at very low freezer temperatures.

(E) Very low, stable freezer temperatures allow for the best possible consistency and flavor of ice cream.

16. Edwina: True appreciation of Mozart's music demands that you hear it exactly as he intended it to be heard; that is, exactly as he heard it. Since he heard it on eighteenth-century instruments, it follows that so should we.

Alberto: But what makes you think that Mozart ever heard his music played as he had intended it to be played? After all, Mozart was writing at a time when the performer was expected, as a matter of course, not just to interpret but to modify the written score.

Alberto adopts which one of the following strategies in criticizing Edwina's position?

(A) He appeals to an academic authority in order to challenge the factual basis of her conclusion.

(B) He attacks her judgment by suggesting that she does not recognize the importance of the performer's creativity to the audience's appreciation of a musical composition.

(C) He defends a competing view of musical authenticity.

(D) He attacks the logic of her argument by suggesting that the conclusion she draws does not follow from the premises she sets forth.

(E) He offers a reason to believe that one of the premises of her argument is false.

GO ON TO THE NEXT PAGE.

17. Since the introduction of the Impanian National Health scheme, Impanians (or their private insurance companies) have had to pay only for the more unusual and sophisticated medical procedures. When the scheme·was introduced, it was hoped that private insurance to pay for these procedures would be available at modest cost, since the insurers would no longer be paying for the bulk of health care costs, as they had done previously. Paradoxically, however, the cost of private health insurance did not decrease but has instead increased dramatically in the years since the scheme's introduction.

Which one of the following, if true, does most to explain the apparently paradoxical outcome?

(A)   The National Health scheme has greatly reduced the number of medical claims handled annually by Impania's private insurers, enabling these firms to reduce overhead costs substantially.

(B)   Before the National Health scheme was introduced, more than 80 percent of all Impanian medical costs were associated with procedures that are now covered by the scheme.

(C)   Impanians who previously were unable to afford regular medical treatment now use the National Health scheme, but the number of Impanians with private health insurance has not increased.

(D)   Impanians now buy private medical insurance only at times when they expect that they will need care of kinds not available in the National Health scheme.

(E)   The proportion of total expenditures within Impania that is spent on health care has declined since the introduction of the National Health scheme.

18. In clinical trials of new medicines, half of the subjects receive the drug being tested and half receive a physiologically inert substance—a placebo. Trials are designed with the intention that neither subjects nor experimenters will find out which subjects are actually being given the drug being tested. However, this intention is frequently frustrated because _____.

Which one of the following, if true, most appropriately completes the explanation?

(A)   often the subjects who receive the drug being tested develop symptoms that the experimenters recognize as side effects of the physiologically active drug

(B)   subjects who believe they are receiving the drug being tested often display improvements in their conditions regardless of whether what is administered to them is physiologically active or not

(C)   in general, when the trial is intended to establish the experimental drug's safety rather than its effectiveness, all of the subjects are healthy volunteers

(D)   when a trial runs a long time, few of the experimenters will work on it from inception to conclusion

(E)   the people who are subjects for clinical trials must, by law, be volunteers and must be informed of the possibility that they will receive a placebo

19. It takes 365.25 days for the Earth to make one complete revolution around the Sun. Long-standing convention makes a year 365 days long, with an extra day added every fourth year, and the year is divided into 52 seven-day weeks. But since 52 times 7 is only 364, anniversaries do not fall on the same day of the week each year. Many scheduling problems could be avoided if the last day of each year and an additional day every fourth year belonged to no week, so that January 1 would be a Sunday every year.

The proposal above, once put into effect, would be most likely to result in continued scheduling conflicts for which one of the following groups?

(A)   people who have birthdays or other anniversaries on December 30 or 31

(B)   employed people whose strict religious observances require that they refrain from working every seventh day

(C)   school systems that require students to attend classes a specific number of days each year

(D)   employed people who have three-day breaks from work when holidays are celebrated on Mondays or Fridays

(E)   people who have to plan events several years before those events occur

GO ON TO THE NEXT PAGE.

20. Graphologists claim that it is possible to detect permanent character traits by examining people's handwriting. For example, a strong cross on the "t" is supposed to denote enthusiasm. Obviously, however, with practice and perseverance people can alter their handwriting to include this feature. So it seems that graphologists must hold that permanent character traits can be changed.

The argument against graphology proceeds by

(A) citing apparently incontestable evidence that leads to absurd consequences when conjoined with the view in question
(B) demonstrating that an apparently controversial and interesting claim is really just a platitude
(C) arguing that a particular technique of analysis can never be effective when the people analyzed know that it is being used
(D) showing that proponents of the view have no theoretical justification for the view
(E) attacking a technique by arguing that what the technique is supposed to detect can be detected quite readily without it

Questions 21–22

Historian: There is no direct evidence that timber was traded between the ancient nations of Poran and Nayal, but the fact that a law setting tariffs on timber imports from Poran was enacted during the third Nayalese dynasty does suggest that during that period a timber trade was conducted.
Critic: Your reasoning is flawed. During its third dynasty, Nayal may well have imported timber from Poran, but certainly on today's statute books there remain many laws regulating activities that were once common but in which people no longer engage.

21. The critic's response to the historian's reasoning does which one of the following?

(A) It implies an analogy between the present and the past.
(B) It identifies a general principle that the historian's reasoning violates.
(C) It distinguishes between what has been established as a certainty and what has been established as a possibility.
(D) It establishes explicit criteria that must be used in evaluating indirect evidence.
(E) It points out the dissimilar roles that law plays in societies that are distinct from one another.

22. The critic's response to the historian is flawed because it

(A) produces evidence that is consistent with there not having been any timber trade between Poran and Nayal during the third Nayalese dynasty
(B) cites current laws without indicating whether the laws cited are relevant to the timber trade
(C) fails to recognize that the historian's conclusion was based on indirect evidence rather than direct evidence
(D) takes no account of the difference between a law's enactment at a particular time and a law's existence as part of a legal code at a particular time
(E) accepts without question the assumption about the purpose of laws that underlies the historian's argument

GO ON TO THE NEXT PAGE.

23. The workers at Bell Manufacturing will shortly go on strike unless the management increases their wages. As Bell's president is well aware, however, in order to increase the workers' wages, Bell would have to sell off some of its subsidiaries. So, some of Bell's subsidiaries will be sold.

The conclusion above is properly drawn if which one of the following is assumed?

(A) Bell Manufacturing will begin to suffer increased losses.
(B) Bell's management will refuse to increase its workers' wages.
(C) The workers at Bell Manufacturing will not be going on strike.
(D) Bell's president has the authority to offer the workers their desired wage increase.
(E) Bell's workers will not accept a package of improved benefits in place of their desired wage increase.

24. One sure way you can tell how quickly a new idea—for example, the idea of "privatization"—is taking hold among the population is to monitor how fast the word or words expressing that particular idea are passing into common usage. Professional opinions of whether or not words can indeed be said to have passed into common usage are available from dictionary editors, who are vitally concerned with this question.

The method described above for determining how quickly a new idea is taking hold relies on which one of the following assumptions?

(A) Dictionary editors are not professionally interested in words that are only rarely used.
(B) Dictionary editors have exact numerical criteria for telling when a word has passed into common usage.
(C) For a new idea to take hold, dictionary editors have to include the relevant word or words in their dictionaries.
(D) As a word passes into common usage, its meaning does not undergo any severe distortions in the process.
(E) Words denoting new ideas tend to be used before the ideas denoted are understood.

25. Because migrant workers are typically not hired by any one employer for longer than a single season, migrant workers can legally be paid less than the minimum hourly wage that the government requires employers to pay all their permanent employees. Yet most migrant workers work long hours each day for eleven or twelve months a year and thus are as much full-time workers as are people hired on a year-round basis. Therefore, the law should require that migrant workers be paid the same minimum hourly wage that other full-time workers must be paid.

The pattern of reasoning displayed above most closely parallels that displayed in which one of the following arguments?

(A) Because day-care facilities are now regulated at the local level, the quality of care available to children in two different cities can differ widely. Since such differences in treatment clearly are unfair, day care should be federally rather than locally regulated.
(B) Because many rural areas have few restrictions on development, housing estates in such areas have been built where no adequate supply of safe drinking water could be ensured. Thus, rural areas should adopt building codes more like those large cities have.
(C) Because some countries regulate gun sales more strictly than do other countries, some people can readily purchase a gun, whereas others cannot. Therefore, all countries should cooperate in developing a uniform international policy regarding gun sales.
(D) Because it is a democratic principle that laws should have the consent of those affected by them, liquor laws should be formulated not by politicians but by club and restaurant owners, since such laws directly affect the profitability of their businesses.
(E) Because food additives are not considered drugs, they have not had to meet the safety standards the government applies to drugs. But food additives can be as dangerous as drugs. Therefore, food additives should also be subject to safety regulations as stringent as those covering drugs.

S T O P

IF YOU FINISH BEFORE TIME IS CALLED, YOU MAY CHECK YOUR WORK ON THIS SECTION ONLY.
DO NOT WORK ON ANY OTHER SECTION IN THE TEST.

SIGNATURE ———————————————————

DATE

LSAT WRITING SAMPLE TOPIC

The city of Stockton must choose an event to inaugurate its new auditorium, an open-air stage with seats for about 15,000 people and a surrounding lawn with room for 30,000 more. Write an argument in favor of hiring either of the following performers with these considerations in mind.

- The city hopes the inaugural performance will raise as much money as possible to pay off the auditorium's construction loans.
- The city wants to obtain considerable positive publicity for the new auditorium.

Astrani, one of the legends of popular music, is giving a farewell concert tour before retiring. He has proposed holding the final three concerts in Stockton; because of his elaborate sets and costumes, tickets would be sold only for the auditorium's seats and no lawn seating would be available. Astrani never allows souvenirs to be sold at his concerts, but the city will receive 20 percent of the proceeds from ticket sales. If the tour ends in Stockton, a well-know director will film the historic event and plans to release a full-length feature which will share the final shows with fans around the world.

A number of prominent bands have organized "Animal-Aid" to raise money for endangered species. The concert has already generated significant attention in the press and a number of important arenas competed for the privilege of hosting the event. Stockton's new auditorium is the organizer's first choice as the site for the all-day concert and the city would be allowed to design and sell souvenirs commemorating the event. While tickets would be available for both the seats and surrounding lawn, all of the proceeds from ticket sales would go to "Animal-Aid." The auditorium's security expert is concerned that the facility's novice staff may not yet have the experience to handle a large crowd during an all-day event.

Directions:

1. Use the Answer Key on the next page to check your answers.

2. Use the Scoring Worksheet below to compute your raw score.

3. Use the Score Conversion Chart to convert your raw score into the 120-180 scale.

Scoring Worksheet

1. Enter the number of questions you answered correctly in each section.

Number
Correct

SECTION I . . . . . . _____
SECTION II . . . . . _____
SECTION III . . . . . _____
SECTION IV . . . . . _____

2. Enter the sum here: _____
This is your Raw Score.

Conversion Chart
Form 3LSS18

For Converting Raw Score to the 120-180 LSAT Scaled Score

Reported Score	Raw Score Lowest	Raw Score Highest
180	98	101
179	97	97
178	95	96
177	94	94
176	93	93
175	92	92
174	91	91
173	90	90
172	89	89
171	88	88
170	86	87
169	85	85
168	84	84
167	82	83
166	81	81
165	79	80
164	78	78
163	76	77
162	75	75
161	73	74
160	72	72
159	70	71
158	68	69
157	67	67
156	65	66
155	64	64
154	62	63
153	60	61
152	59	59
151	57	58
150	56	56
149	54	55
148	53	53
147	51	52
146	50	50
145	48	49
144	47	47
143	45	46
142	44	44
141	42	43
140	41	41
139	39	40
138	38	38
137	37	37
136	35	36
135	34	34
134	33	33
133	31	32
132	30	30
131	29	29
130	28	28
129	27	27
128	26	26
127	24	25
126	23	23
125	22	22
124	21	21
123	20	20
122	19	19
121	18	18
120	0	17

SECTION I

1.	C	8.	A	15.	A	22.	E
2.	C	9.	D	16.	B	23.	D
3.	E	10.	B	17.	B	24.	A
4.	E	11.	C	18.	C	25.	D
5.	B	12.	A	19.	C		
6.	E	13.	C	20.	B		
7.	C	14.	E	21.	B		

SECTION II

1.	C	8.	B	15.	E	22.	D
2.	A	9.	C	16.	A	23.	B
3.	C	10.	E	17.	E	24.	A
4.	C	11.	E	18.	B		
5.	E	12.	E	19.	E		
6.	C	13.	B	20.	D		
7.	D	14.	C	21.	B		

SECTION III

1.	E	8.	D	15.	B	22.	C
2.	D	9.	A	16.	D	23.	D
3.	C	10.	B	17.	C	24.	E
4.	B	11.	C	18.	E	25.	B
5.	D	12.	C	19.	A	26.	B
6.	A	13.	E	20.	D	27.	D
7.	A	14.	D	21.	C		

SECTION IV

1.	D	8.	E	15.	E	22.	D
2.	E	9.	C	16.	E	23.	C
3.	B	10.	D	17.	D	24.	D
4.	E	11.	A	18.	A	25.	E
5.	A	12.	A	19.	B		
6.	C	13.	D	20.	A		
7.	A	14.	D	21.	A		